THREE FILMS BY INGMAR BERGMAN

THREE FILMS
BY
INGMAR BERGMAN

Through A Glass Darkly
Winter Light
The Silence

Translated by Paul Britten Austin

Grove Press, Inc. New York

Originally published in Swedish as *En Filmtrilogi by*
P. A. Norstedt and Söners Förlag, Stockholm, 1963.

ISBN: 0-394-17281-7
Grove Press ISBN: 0-8021-4077-7

Library of Congress Catalog Card Number: 67-21231

First Evergreen Edition 1970
Sixth Printing 1977

Manufactured in the United States of America

DISTRIBUTED BY RANDOM HOUSE, INC., NEW YORK

GROVE PRESS, INC., 196 WEST HOUSTON STREET,
NEW YORK, N.Y., 10014

The theme of these three films is a 'reduction'—
in the metaphysical sense of that word.

THROUGH A GLASS DARKLY–certainty
achieved.

WINTER LIGHT–certainty unmasked.

THE SILENCE–God's silence–the **negative**
impression.

Stockholm, May, 1963.

Ingmar Bergman.

Contents

All the photographs in this book are reproduced with the kind permission of Janus Films.

THROUGH A GLASS DARKLY

Rättvik
May 12, 1960

To Käbi
my wife

Through a Glass Darkly

I

The house, strongly marked by its exposed position, stands by itself on a long sandy promontory. Built in two storys, it is a dark green color, except where sun and wind have burnished its timbers to a lighter silky hue. At the back it looks out over a large wild garden, all run to seed and partly screened from prying eyes by a high paling.

People are living in the house. Washing flaps on the line, and underneath ragged and wind-blown awnings the windows are wide open.

Out of heaving waves, half-dark in the gloaming, arise shouts and laughter. Suddenly four heads are bobbing on the waves, and after a moment four people begin struggling in through the shallows, toward the shore. They are breathing hard, as if after a long swim, and laugh helplessly as they walk side by side—four black figures against the sunset, whose troubled fires dart and gleam, mirrored in the waves.

Two men, a boy and a woman.

They clamber up the long wooden jetty, shattered by winter ice, and wrap themselves in towels and bathing gowns. Already there's a nip in the evening breeze, though in the water it's quite mild and warm.

KARIN: Daddy and Martin lay the net out, and Minus and I'll fetch the milk.

MARTIN: This evening I think David and Minus should put out the net, so I can take a stroll with my wife.

DAVID: Can't Karin and I put it out and Minus and Martin fetch the milk?

MINUS: I've no intention either of fetching the milk or laying out any nets. I'll decide for myself what I'm going to do.

KARIN: Come along now, Minus. You and I'll go. We haven't had a glimpse of each other all day.

MARTIN: Why've women always got to have the last word?

DAVID: I decide . . . that we do what Karin's decided. Then we haven't lost our dignity. And that's the main thing.

KARIN: Think how much time we'd have saved if Daddy'd thought of that to begin with.

They all laugh amicably together and go in Indian file up towards the house: David first, then Fredrik (or Minus); Karin; and Martin last.

Minus climbs in through the window, Karin disappears in the direction of the kitchen. David and Martin light their pipes, contemplating the sunset.

DAVID: Shall we go in and put something on or lay the net out at once? What d'you think?

MARTIN: What do you think?

DAVID: Getting a little chilly, don't you think?

MARTIN: Think so?

DAVID: My wrap's thinner than yours.

MARTIN: Well, of course, if you're cold.

DAVID: Me? Not in the least! Are you?

MARTIN: Me? It was you who said it was cold. I must say there's quite a nip in the breeze, though.

DAVID: We'll toughen up. Virility comes before health, eh?

MARTIN: What's Hemingway got that we haven't! So—forward!

They feint like boxers and make off for the fishermen's huts where the nets have been hung up to dry.

Minus puts on a pair of old worn jeans and an outsize thick sweater, combing his hair in the latest style in front of a cracked boy's-room mirror. Then hops out of the window.

Stands and bawls for Karin.

Getting no answer, he scurries round the corner of the house and pops up outside her window, is just about to shout again, but doesn't.

Inside, half-averted, Karin, quite naked, is standing drying herself with a big bath-towel. She bends down, turns and twists as she rubs herself down. Catching sight of him, she smiles and flings the towel at his face and a wet, pungent darkness overwhelms him as he grabs it in his hands. Careless of her brother's gaze, Karin dresses, runs a comb through her wet hair and takes a thick sweater out of her wardrobe.

She nods to Minus, who vanishes beneath the window-sill and stumbles away through the rose bushes. They meet again outside the kitchen door, where the milk jug lies overturned on the steps.

Karin takes hold of her brother by his shoulders and together they set out; first through the garden, then into the wood. The farm lies on the far side of the island.

The sun has set into opaque masses of cloud. Twilight begins to fall. To the east, far out to sea, a thunderstorm is gathering; in the dark violet wall of the cloud-mass lightning flashes soundlessly and makes sharp

scratches. Now the lighthouse begins to fling its white jabs of light across shore and water. The evening breeze dies away, and the sea-birds fall silent and sweep dark and anxious over the long swell of the sea.
David and Martin carry down the net.

DAVID: Think there'll be thunder?

MARTIN: Not tonight.

DAVID: Take a look at those clouds.

MARTIN: What, frightened of thunder?

DAVID: Scared to death. Can't control it. In Switzerland . . . when it rolled about among those bloody Alps . . . hell!

MARTIN: Otherwise you enjoyed yourself down there?

DAVID: I was homesick. But I'd sworn not to come home till the novel was finished.

MARTIN: And now it is.

DAVID: Yes, thanks. More or less.

MARTIN: How's the ulcer?

DAVID: Not too bad. You'll have to prescribe something. The change of climate's bad for it.

MARTIN: We'll take the car in to the chemist tomorrow. There are several things I must attend to, anyway.

They go down towards the beach, Martin carrying the net over his shoulder. David fetches the oars from the boathouse.

MARTIN: Tell me, did you get my last letter? I posted it on Monday.

DAVID: I was at the Waldsteins' in Zurich. They send their regards.

MARTIN: Then I suppose you didn't get my letter.

DAVID: On Wednesday I took the plane straight home.

MARTIN: Then you can't have had it.

DAVID: Something wrong?

MARTIN: It was about Karin.

David, who has been busy bailing out the boat, straightens his back and throws a troubled glance at Martin, who is still standing on the jetty, the net flung over his shoulder.

DAVID: About Karin? What about Karin?

MARTIN: Well, I don't know. But I felt I had to drop you a line. Even if it disturbed you in the very act of creation.

Martin's tone of voice is faintly ironical, he steps down into the boat and seats himself at the oars. David scrutinizes his pipe, which is going out, stuffs it in the pocket of his bathing wrap, casts off the mooring rope.

17

Karin and Minus are hurrying on their way through the wood in the gloaming. Suddenly they stop and listen.

KARIN: Quiet!

MINUS: What?

KARIN: It was a cuckoo. Can't you hear?

MINUS: No.

KARIN: Yes. Now. You must hear it.

MINUS: Where?

KARIN: There.

MINUS: Still can't hear.

KARIN: When did my little brother last wash his ears, may I ask?

MINUS: Oh, shut up. It's you who hear too much.

KARIN: Yes, it's true. It's very odd, but since my illness my hearing has become so sensitive. Maybe it was the electro-shocks, I can't say. Sudden loud noises send me out of my wits.

MINUS: Now I can hear it, too.

They begin walking again, but more slowly.

KARIN: How d'you think Daddy looked yesterday when he came back from Switzerland?

MINUS: Looked?

KARIN: Quite gay, I thought.

MINUS: Must have been tired after travelling.

KARIN: Yes.

MINUS: He doesn't seem particularly happy.

KARIN: D'you know if Marianne's coming here this summer?

MINUS: I think they've broken it off. Martin mumbled something to that effect.

KARIN: Poor Daddy. So he's all alone again.

MINUS: I never liked Marianne!

KARIN: She made so much fuss about herself and her superiority, Daddy became quite simple and straightforward by comparison. She turned her nose up at his books, too.

Again Karin puts her arm round her brother. It's rather uncomfortable since he's tall and walks brusquely with an impatient gait.

MINUS: Daddy's just got to succeed with this book. He *must* get good reviews.

KARIN: But surely everyone's reading his novels?

MINUS: That's not what matters. He doesn't give two hoots

18

how many copies he sells. What he wants is to be regarded as a genius, don't you see that?

Karin stops, frees herself from Minus, stands face to face with him, and looks him between the eyes. Then she begins to laugh.

MINUS: What are you giggling at?

KARIN: At you, of course. Because you're so tall. And so serious. "He wants to be regarded as a *genius*, don't you see?" (*Laughs*) And no need to put on such an air of injured innocence! I love you, little Minus. But it's *horrible* how tall you've grown.

MINUS: Don't be an ass.

KARIN: Fifteen, and nearly seven foot tall. And where's *your* girl-friend, eh?

MINUS: Who the hell do you imagine would want to go out with me?

Karin laughs again and takes him by the arm, drags him after her, and throws a sidelong glance at his soft impatient features.

KARIN: No need to be grumpy because I laughed at you.

MINUS: I can't stand being laughed at.

KARIN (*softly*): Forgive me, then.

MINUS: You needn't apologize. I know I'm ridiculous and everyone's got the right to laugh at me. It's good for me.

KARIN: In my opinion Daddy *is* a genius.

MINUS: No, that's just what he isn't. And never will be. Though he can't see it himself.

Karin shakes her head, but doesn't reply. They hasten their footsteps. Around them the forest grows darker. Somewhere in the distance thunder rumbles. Karin stops.

KARIN: Oh, no, no, no. No.

MINUS (*softly*): What is it?

KARIN: No, no. Nothing.

MINUS: Sure?

KARIN: No, nothing. Don't be scared. It's nothing. (*Pause*) Can you hear the thunder . . .?

MINUS: Sure.

Karin stands on tiptoe and kisses her brother on his ear. Then they hurry on. Martin is rowing round the point, into the stillness of the creek. David is sitting, leaning forward, the net in his hand.

MARTIN: Edgar's the only psychiatrist I've any faith in. He's been looking after her all the time. D'you know him?

DAVID (*nods*): Well?

MARTIN: When Karin came home from the hospital, a month ago now, he and I discussed the whole thing in detail.

DAVID (*glances at him*).

MARTIN: He couldn't promise any lasting improvement.

DAVID: And now?

MARTIN: It seems unusually O.K. She sleeps a bit restlessly at nights and her hearing has become so oversensitive.

DAVID: What does she know?

MARTIN: Well, really everything. Except that it's more or less incurable.

DAVID: More or less, you say.

MARTIN: Edgar's had cases which have made a complete recovery. So there's always hope.

DAVID: And yourself, how are you keeping?

MARTIN: Not so bad.

DAVID: That's a short answer.

MARTIN: I was wondering just how interested you are?

DAVID: A good question. (*Gives a short laugh.*)

MARTIN: The days pass. All the spring I've had my lectures at the polytechnic and examined a hell of a crowd of students. Then I've moved my practice and got myself a bit more space. But I think I told you that in one of my letters.

He falls silent, looks at his hands as they grip the oars.

DAVID: And Minus?

MARTIN: He's got his own troubles.

Silence again. Far out to sea a boat blows its siren. Beyond the creek's stillness the waves are breaking on the shore.

DAVID: It's hard to talk.

MARTIN: Yes, it's hard. When Karin got ill we were what is called happy. Before I realized the whole extent of the catastrophe both she and I were just about at the end of our tether.

DAVID: You hinted at something of the sort in your letters.

MARTIN: Not much. After all, you were busy with your novel. I didn't want to upset you.

DAVID (*silent, looks away*): Sure.

MARTIN: I've come to understand that I love her and can't help being part of her, whatever happens. I'm all she has to cling to in life, her only security perhaps.

DAVID: I understand.

MARTIN: She says I'm her only defense against the disease. Maybe she's right.

Silence.

MARTIN: Shall we put the net out?

DAVID: Just what I was thinking.

David begins to let the net down into the black water while Martin rows cautiously ahead. Now and again the sound of distant thunder rolls across the sea.

The spot of light from the lighthouse has grown whiter and harder.

Minus and Karin leave the farm, whose buildings stand out in sharp black silhouette against the lighter darkness of the sky. Above the horizon hangs the chill crescent of the moon. The thundery weather to the north slowly moves eastward.

Minus is carrying the milk jug. Karin has broken off a branch and is swatting midges. Far away across the fields, which lie softly beneath exhalations of light mist, a corncrake's cry is heard.

The night is cloudy yet almost white and the forest swarms with life.

They turn off from the path and try to find a way down to the shore.

Minus gives a deep sigh, turns a pale face toward Karin and suddenly flings himself down full-length on the ground, biting his fingernails.

KARIN: What's troubling you?

MINUS (*no answer*).

KARIN: What's the matter, Minus?

She sits down beside him and patiently waits for him to come to himself.

MINUS: The walls in the house are so thin, and I can't help hearing when you and Martin are making love, it drives me mad, can't you go and do it somewhere else?

KARIN (*silent*).

MINUS: You'd better look out. Keep away from me. And stop kissing and hugging me all the time. Don't lie there half-naked when you're sunbathing, it makes me feel sick to see you.

KARIN: Minus! What d'you mean?

MINUS (*angry*): You know very well what I mean. Women are the bloody limit. They smell and stick their stomachs out and make special sorts of movements and comb their hair and gossip—till you feel like a skinned rabbit.

KARIN: Poor chap.

MINUS: That's right! Thanks very much!—Pity! I can supply myself with as much of that commodity as I need.

He presses his forehead into the sand and hunches his shoulders, hiding his cheeks and ears with his hands. Karin snuggles up beside him, bringing her face close to his. She speaks very softly and gently, as to a baby, patiently and indistinctly. After a while he sits up. The tension has begun to wear off.

MINUS: Don't go and tell Martin or Daddy will know.

KARIN: Now you're being really silly.

MINUS: Oh, look. Now I've gone and spilt the milk, too.

Troubled, he looks down at the milk jug, which is lying on its side in the sand. Karin takes it and gets up.

KARIN: Come on, Minus.

MINUS: Think, if for just once in my life I could talk to Daddy. But he's so absorbed in his own affairs. (*Pause. He adds*) Him too.

Karin doesn't answer, walks with her own thoughts.

It is still quite warm in the garden, the house affords shelter from the sea-breezes and its walls emanate warmth from the summer sunshine. Under a tree David and Martin have laid the supper table and hung up some lanterns in its branches.

Martin cuts his finger on the top of a bottle, sticks his finger in his mouth, takes it out again and looks glumly at the drop of blood gathering there.

MARTIN: There's nothing I hate so much as cutting the tip of my finger.

DAVID: Put a band-aid on.

Minus and Karin come in from the forest.

MINUS: Hello. What are you up to?

MARTIN: Hello.

DAVID: Martin's cut his finger.

KARIN: Let me see.

Martin holds out his finger. Karin sucks the blood, looks at it, sucks again, is suddenly all enthusiasm.

KARIN: It seems a deep cut. Hadn't we better put a band-aid on?

MARTIN: What a hell of a fuss over a finger.

DAVID: Well? Don't you think we've arranged it all nicely, supper and lanterns, under the new moon?

MINUS: I'll just put the milk in the cellar.

David has come out with a stew-pot, steaming with delicious odours. He lifts the lid. Cries of admiration.

KARIN: You're a master of the art of cookery, Daddy.

MARTIN: A most remarkable odour.

MINUS (*calls from the cellar*): Wait for me.

Minus comes out to the others and with a deep breath inhales the aroma, makes an ecstatic face and pats his stomach.

MINUS: Daddy! Why don't you write cook books instead of novels?

They all laugh, a shade too brightly, and sit down to table. David serves up the food out of the stew-pot. Martin pours out some beer. Karin cuts the bread. Minus takes some potatoes for himself out of the casserole.

MARTIN: Well, *skal*, David. And welcome home.

They clink glasses, drink beer.

DAVID: If you only knew how I've been longing for this moment.

MINUS: Have you? Why?

DAVID: I was homesick every minute I was away.

MINUS: Homesick for us?

DAVID: Even for you.

MINUS: And are you going to stay now?

DAVID: This month, anyway.

KARIN: What! You aren't going away *again*!

DAVID: Yes, surely I must have told you? I'm going to take a party of tourists to Yugoslavia. It'll be a . . .

KARIN: A party of tourists! But what on earth for?

DAVID: A most flattering offer. It's one of those cultural delegations, you know. And since I know the country—well, why not?

MINUS: And what about your book?

DAVID: Oh that. That'll be finished before. I've spoken to the publishers. I'm handing in the whole typescript next week.

MARTIN: How long'll you be away?

DAVID: Don't know really. Maybe I'll stay on awhile at Dubrovnik, after the others have gone home.

A moment's silence follows. David looks from one to the other, then laughs.

DAVID: Somehow or other I feel like a criminal.

MINUS: You promised you'd stay home after Switzerland. Didn't you?

DAVID: I've a vague memory we . . . we spoke of it. But that I ever promised . . .

MINUS: You promised, Daddy.

DAVID: What a shame.

MINUS: Yes, it's a shame.

Silence again. Suddenly Karin leans forward and pats David's hand.

KARIN: We were going to have such fun this evening and now we're almost crying.

David laughs with embarrassment and gives his daughter a hasty kiss on her hand.

DAVID: By the way, I've brought you all presents from Switzerland. Wait a moment, I'll show you.

He dives under the table and fetches out three packets, which he hands to them. The presents are opened, their wrapping paper unfolded. David looks around, as if seeking help, then gets up from the table.

DAVID: Excuse me, I'll just fetch my baccy.

Minus sits with a watch in his hand. Karin has received a pair of elegant gloves, too small for her, and Martin is undoing an electric razor.

As soon as David is out of earshot Minus makes his comment.

MINUS: I'd bet my life Daddy only thought of presents when he was back in Stockholm.

KARIN: It was kind of him, anyway.

MINUS: I'd sooner have had the money.

David hurries into his room, closes the door and stands breathlessly in the middle of the floor, looks around him as if at a loss, or searching for something. Walks round the room, touches various objects, begins to sob, drily, as if hiccuping, takes a deep breath, begins to cry more violently, bangs his fist again and again on the table, trying to suppress the despair that is overwhelming him.

Finally he controls himself, finds his tobacco tin, puts it under his arm, blows his nose and wipes his eyes.

Then he returns to the table. Everyone is very tactful. Expressions of gratitude are heaped upon him.

He sits down and stuffs his pipe, slides the tin over to Martin and gives an embarrassed smile.

KARIN: We've got a surprise for you, too, Daddy.

DAVID: How terribly nice of you.

MINUS: But we'll have to blindfold you and lead you over to the summerhouse.

KARIN: Don't look till we tell you.

David, relieved and smiling, lets himself be blindfolded. Then he is led across the garden to its most dilapidated corner, where an ancient summerhouse is gradually falling into ruin. Here Minus has nailed a few planks together to make a primitive stage. The end of a bed forms one end and a decayed pear tree the other. The crumbling doors of the summerhouse are open and inside in the darkness flicker three candles. The stage itself is lit by three paraffin lamps—which act as footlights. Backstage the leafy greenery of the garden grows thickly, and here and there one catches a glimpse of the evening sky and the sea. Moths flutter against the lanterns, throwing shadows against the white walls of the summerhouse.

David has been placed in an old plush sofa whose bottom is coming out, and the blindfold is removed from his eyes. Martin sits down under the pear tree, guitar in hand.

He strikes a few chords.

Minus appears, dressed in a dark cape, his face blackened with a soot moustache, a sword at his side. Out of the darkness of the summerhouse resound twelve dull blows on the house-gong.

Martin turns to David and speaks with a politely disguised voice.

MARTIN: Our drama is called "The Artistic Haunting" or, "The Funeral Vault of Illusions" and is not composed to delight a big public. It is a morality play, intended only for poets and authors.—Let the play commence.

Minus unfreezes from his immobile posture and steps forward to the footlights.

MINUS: The clock has struck twelve in the chapel of Saint Theresa. The night is still and starless. Here in this funeral vault, breathing death's perfumes, I have been permitted to meet her, my heart's betrothed.

Martin strikes a few chords on his guitar. The lights inside the summerhouse flicker in a sudden draught. Then all is still again.

MINUS. Something stirred within. Perhaps it is she. I will hide, not to affright her.

He goes behind the screen. Martin strikes another chord, this time weird, doleful. In the doorway Karin is glimpsed, vanishes, returns. She steps out onto the stage.

Her hair is combed back and on her head she is wearing a little crown of silver paper. Round her shoulders she has swept a large black shawl; she is very pale, an effect still further heightened by eye-shadow. In one hand she is holding a wooden sceptre. Ceremoniously she steps forward toward the footlights but, catching sight of Minus behind the screen, hesitates:

MINUS: Who are you?

KARIN: I am a princess of Castille, dead in childbirth in my thirteenth year. My husband is the same age. He was my playmate and my belovèd lord. Now his thoughts have turned to other women.

25

MINUS: Yet he mourns you?

KARIN: He was inconsolable. Every morning he stepped down into my tomb, weeping there all day. In the evening they must needs carry him back to the castle. Suddenly, one day, he came no more. A servant wench had consoled him so completely he had overslept. Thereafter he grieved but one hour a day, and now only pays me a courtesy visit on alternate Sundays. His eyes are dry and his thoughts elsewhere.

MINUS: Princess, I love you!

KARIN: I thank you for your kindness. But who are you, anyway? Surely you understand I cannot speak to any Tom, Dick or Harry, dead though I be.

MINUS: Have no fear, sweet lady. In my own kingdom, poor though it is and not large, I am a king. I am an artist.

KARIN: An artist?

MINUS: In sooth, Princess. I am an artist of purest blood. A poet without poems, a painter without paintings, a musician without music, even an actor without a role. The completed work, banal fruit of simple-minded strivings, I despise. My life is my lifework; and it is dedicated to my love for you, Princess.

KARIN: That sounds beautiful but incredible.

MINUS: I prithee, put me to the proof.

Karin, smiling sadly, goes up to Minus, who falls on his knee. Martin calls forth three frail notes from his instrument. Karin also falls on her knees before her artist.

KARIN: Hear and attend. In a few moments I shall leave you. When the monastery bell strikes twice, step down into the burial vault and snuff the three lights which burn faintly therein. At that moment the doors will close for ever; you will follow me into the realm of death. What shall happen thereafter is hid; yet I swear to remain at your side for ever and ever.

MINUS: The sacrifice is easy, Princess. What is life to a *real* artist?

She raises her hands to his face and gazes at him a long while, speaking with sudden melancholy, sprung, as it were, from a double sorrow.

KARIN: In this way you will complete your masterpiece and crown your love; ennoble your life and show to those of little faith what a true artist can achieve. Farewell, my friend. Do not fail me!

Martin plays his fragile melody. Slowly, Karin disappears into the darkness of the summerhouse.

MINUS: I am standing on the threshold of an ultimate consummation! I tremble with excitement. Oblivion shall possess me and only death shall love me.

Out of the darkness of the summerhouse the gong strikes dully, twice.

MINUS: So—I go. Nothing can restrain me.

He turns to the door, but suddenly hesitates, clasps his head in his hands.

KARIN (*within*): I'm waiting.

MINUS: Holy Mother of God, what is it roaring inside my head, clutching at my throat and thudding deep down in my stomach?

KARIN (*as before*): I'm waiting.

MINUS: In the name of all the devils! What am I about? Sacrificing my life! For what? For eternity. To the perfect masterpiece. For love! Am I out of my mind?

KARIN: I'm waiting.

MINUS: My knees are clay. I tremble in every limb. My stomach is behaving most improperly, and I can't enter eternity with . . .

KARIN (*sadly*): Now I'm not waiting any more.

The doors of the summerhouse close with a bang. The lights inside go out and silence falls. Minus shrugs his shoulders.

MINUS: Naturally, I could write a poem about my meeting with the princess. Or paint a picture, or compose an opera. Though the end, of course, must be given a more heroic twist. Let me see: Oblivion shall claim me and only death shall love me. That's not bad.

Minus lays his finger on his nose. Somewhere inside, Karin crows like a cock.

MINUS: The cocks of morning forbode the dawn. (*Yawns*) I'll go home and sleep on it. Truly I could do with a little sleep.

Minus disappears yawning behind the screen. The cock crows again in the bushes.

MINUS (*behind the screen*): Well, that's all.

David feels he should applaud. Martin helps as best he can. Karin comes out on to the stage and bows deeply, in the manner of actors.

DAVID (*shouts*):   Author! Author!
Karin brings out Minus, who holds back reluctantly, in the manner of authors. At the same time he gives a big slightly self-conscious smile. David gets up from the bench and clasps the artistes' hands. Martin picks up two of the paraffin lamps and Karin takes the third. Happily chatting, the party go up toward the house.
KARIN: Now, everyone give a hand to clear away and wash up, so we'll get it over quickly.
DAVID: I'll see to that. I shan't be able to get to sleep for hours yet, anyway.
MARTIN: Out of the question.
DAVID: I'll enjoy having something to do for an hour or so. So you're doing me a favour.
KARIN (*laughs*):   Oh very well, then—we won't insist.
They all say good-night to each other. Minus is praised again for his drama. Martin goes inside the house with the paraffin lamps.
DAVID: D'you feel how soft the air is? It'll certainly be nice weather tomorrow.
MINUS: The thunder's gone over.
KARIN: As I said all along.
MARTIN (*looks out*):   Who's left the window open? The bedroom's swarming with midges. That's a fine thing!
MINUS: What do a few midges matter?
KARIN: Good-night, then, Daddy.
DAVID: Good-night, Karin.
MINUS: Good-night all.
In the quietness of the almost unstirring night they exchange a few words. David has sat down at the table and is smoking his pipe. He sees how Karin and Martin are preparing for the night. In his room, on the other side of the hall, Minus has lit a lamp. He pulls down a tattered blind. David gives a little sigh and begins gathering up the dirty dishes.
Martin is lying on top of his bed, dressed in a pair of old, faded, and rather shrunken pyjamas, which have no buttons to their jacket. He has shoved his glasses up on to his forehead and is totally absorbed in clipping the fingernails of his right hand. Karin is doing odd jobs about the room, dragging articles of clothing about after her. Now and again Martin throws a glance in her direction.
MARTIN: Give me a hand, will you?
Karin comes up to the bed, sits down, and takes his hand, inspecting each nail in turn.

28

KARIN: How dirty they get when you potter about in the garden. And it won't go away.

She is turned toward the lamp, her back bowed and her toes splayed out in her sandals. Martin kisses her shoulder and yawns.

KARIN: Really you've very kind fingers. All soft and good-natured. And the little finger quite childish; only the thumb looks stubborn.

MARTIN: Are you unhappy, Karin?

KARIN: No, not really.

MARTIN: What are you thinking?

KARIN: Sometimes one is so defenseless—Well, maybe not, I don't know.

MARTIN *(looks at her).*

KARIN: Like children exposed in the desert at night. The owls come flying by and look at you out of their yellow eyes. There are paddings and rustlings and soughings and sighings. And all the damp noses nosing. And wolves' teeth.

MARTIN: But we have each other, haven't we, you and I?

KARIN: I don't know, you look so anxious.

MARTIN *(laughs):* No, really. I'm not anxious.

KARIN: You say there aren't any wolves, after all I can't see them, and no owl, either, I can't hear a sound, and all that about the wolf is pure imagination.

MARTIN: Rely on me. Karin. Dear little Kajsa.

He takes her by the shoulders and turns her face towards him, trying to catch her glance. At first she avoids him but afterwards she looks at him a long while, ironically.

KARIN: Dear little Kajsa. You always say that. Little Kajsa. Am I so little or is it my illness has turned me into a child? Do you mean there's something odd about me?

MARTIN: D'you believe I'm telling the truth?

KARIN: I don't know.

She checks herself and looks away. Martin takes his glasses down from off his brow and sets them straight; takes the scissors from Karin and begins clipping the fingernails of his left hand.

MARTIN: Don't you believe I love you?

KARIN *(nods):* Yes. I believe it.

MARTIN: Isn't it enough?

KARIN: Oh yes. It's enough.

Suddenly she is deeply and tragically miserable. Martin becomes more and more irresolute, suddenly begins tugging at the band-aid on his forefinger.

KARIN: Don't do that. It'll start bleeding again.

MARTIN: It'll be all right.

Again, Karin begins wandering round the room, in a planless troubled way.

KARIN: Got to do the washing tomorrow, anyway.

MARTIN: Come to bed now, Karin.

KARIN: Didn't you notice how Daddy took Minus's little play as a personal affront? It hurt his feelings badly, though he tried not to show it.

MARTIN: Think so?

KARIN (*nods*): And Minus was upset, of course.

In the end Karin goes to bed, snuggles up to Martin, lays her head on his shoulder, he strokes her arm and her back.

KARIN: Shall we put the light out?

Martin disentangles himself, but stops and turns to her, leans over her and begins kissing her very tenderly.

KARIN (*humbly*): I'm sorry if I upset you.

MARTIN: Darling little Kajsa.

KARIN: Forgive me.

MARTIN: Dearest, beloved. Dearest, dearest heart. I love you. You can never upset me.

KARIN (*whispers*): You're so kind and I'm so nasty.

Martin reaches out his hand and strangles the flame of the paraffin lamp. It gutters and gutters. At last it's gone.

Far off, but clearly, one hears the surge of the sea. A blackbird is already beginning to whistle in the oak tree outside the windows.

Minus tosses and turns in his bed, throws off his blankets, flings the pillow on to the floor, sits up, lies down again, screws his eyes tight shut, pulls the sheet over his face; but nothing is any good. The tattered blind rustles, the blackbird whistles. Now and then he hears voices from the bedroom. Finally he throws off the sheet, puts his feet into his shoes, pulls his sweater over his head and jumps out of the window.

Then he rushes down to the fisherman's hut. After hunting around inside for a while, he comes out with his sleeping bag and unrolls it at the far end of the jetty.

Then he sees David coming toward him.

DAVID: Too warm for you?

MINUS: It's nicer sleeping outdoors.

*Minus creeps down into his sleeping bag. David stands a little farther off
on the jetty and looks down into the water.*

DAVID: Minus?

MINUS: Yes, Daddy.

DAVID: Do you despise me?

MINUS: No. Why?

DAVID: I have my suspicions.

MINUS: Sometimes I'd like to . . .

DAVID: Yes?

MINUS: Nothing. Are you going to work tonight?

DAVID (*nods*): I find it rather hard to sleep, anyway.

MINUS: 'Bye then.

DAVID: Good-night, Minus. Sleep tight.

*David nods to his son, and walks slowly up toward the house. Minus's
gaze follows him. Now the paraffin lamp is lit in the study.*

*It's just before sunrise, a damp expectant silence. The sea sleeps restlessly,
the sky heavy with rain. On the horizon to the east a blood-red streak of
sky is afire.*

*Karin, who has been sleeping beside her husband, awakes abruptly, all
ears, as if someone were calling her.*

*She sits up in bed and looks round. It's already light in the room, the
flimsy curtains at the windows haven't even been drawn. Martin is sleeping
soundly, he has turned his back to her and lies bunched up with his knees
drawn up and one hand under his cheek.*

*His face, as he sleeps, seems childlike, almost simple-minded. His
breathing, through the half-open mouth, is scarcely audible.*

*Karin listens for the voice. But it is silent now. From the grey morning
sea comes the hungry cry of a seabird. Her wrist watch shows a quarter
past three, her heart thuds irregularly and the old house is full of creakings
and groanings, as if cautiously stirring in its sleep.*

*She drinks a glass of water, lies down on her back again, stares at the
ceiling. One hand seeks out her husband, rests against his shoulder.*

*But she can find no peace. She sits up again, runs both her hands through
her hair and gets out of bed.*

*She swathes herself in a sun-faded bathing robe, shuffles on her slippers
and silently glides out of the room.*

*In the hallway, where the stairs go up, and where a window looks out into
the garden, it is still half twilight. The huge grandfather clock leans
uneasily against the wall and the iron stove turns its face away in rusty
self-pity, while a shapeless sofa in heavy art nouveau style stretches itself*

31

out in the floating uncertain light. It's cold out here, a damp·musty air of old wood and a house that's dying.

The stairs creak at every step and the red rail of the banisters, with its ornamental carvings, sways slightly.

The upper floor has a large landing, which at one time served as a sitting-room; peculiarly-shaped monsters, furniture, sleep here beneath white sheeting, like prehistoric creatures, long dead beneath the snow. None of these upper rooms is occupied; either they have fallen into decay or else preserved themselves without any outside attention whatever. The ceiling is stained, strange fantastic patterns resembling charts of unknown seas; the linoleum on the floor has been ripped up in great open sores, rotting planks have collapsed or been broken up, revealing the fillings in walls and floors. The wallpapers are damp-stained and sun-bleached; here and there they have come up in great blisters or else sag loose, hanging from the walls in strips.

In the hall Karin hesitates, but then goes into the room which looks out toward the sunrise. She tries to close the door behind her but the frame has warped and the lock is broken.

Apart from an old Windsor chair and a little nursery table, this room is void of furniture. The floor, which once consisted of clean-scrubbed boards, has been partially ripped up and the floorboards are propped against the wall. What immediately strikes the eye in this room, however, is its wallpaper. Green in color, it is really supposed to represent leaves in various shades, tones and tinges. In some spots the color has faded completely and the pattern appears only very faint and grey; but in the corners and behind the pictures the foliage is still strong and leafy. In the wall to the right of the window is a narrow door, also covered with wallpaper, above which a patch of damp has exploded and given birth to a laughing moon-face with one dud eye, a gaping mouth and a huge potato nose. To the left of the window, over the whole width of one strip, the pattern of leaves has been ripped away, and behind it a stiff brownish composition with fading golden edges has come into view.

Karin has come to a halt in the middle of the room; her posture is one of petrified attentiveness, as if expecting to hear someone speak to her. She has let go of her dressing-gown and holds her hand out motionlessly before her; her head is turned to one side and her gaze is fixed on the right-hand wall.

Suddenly, small flames of fire are alight in the heavy petals of the wall-paper, a convulsive puff of wind comes from the sea and the house sighs like an old ship with its masts and rigging.

32

*The disc of the sun comes rolling out of the grey ocean swell and little
orange tongues of fire flicker over the wallpaper's leafy designs.
Karin gives a sigh, breathes deeply; a sound, as of repressed singing or
whispering, stirs in her throat. Her face swells and darkens and her eyes
become glazed, unaware.
Slowly, she sinks down on her knees, legs wide apart.
David has been leaning over the manuscript of his novel, turning its pages
to and fro. He has opened the window toward the sea, and for long periods
has stood staring out into the unreal, mysterious twilit dawn. He has been
smoking incessantly, his eyes burn feverishly, every nerve in his body is
tense, he tries to fight off a faint feeling of sickness.
The compact piles of typewritten pages (with rewritten and corrected
passages, changes and additions in red ink) are lying on his writing desk.
Otherwise, there are few pieces of furniture in his room—a narrow camp
bed, a bookshelf with a few books in a half-empty row, a stand with its
basin and jug behind a screen, a rocking chair and a couple of other hard
wooden chairs.
He leans his head against a windowpane and feels his pulse. Yes, he must
have a temperature, he'd better take a couple of aspirins. He searches on
the bookshelf, above the washstand, among pillboxes and bottles.
Grey, chilled by the morning, he sits down on the edge of his bed and tries
to swallow the tablets. The sunrise has already been doused behind the
mighty rainclouds above the sea, the room is filled with a hard daylight
which throws all contours into sharp relief.
David puts his hand to his chest and breathes deeply and with difficulty;
then he gets up and goes over to his writing desk and the heaps of typewritten pages, with their multitudes of red scars.*

DAVID (*reads*): She came toward him, panting with expectation,
scarlet-faced in the keen wind . . . (*sighs*) Oh my God, oh
my God.

*He thrusts his spectacles up on his brow and hides his grey face in his
hands. But after a few moments he resumes work.*

DAVID (*reads*): She came toward him, panting with expectation . . .

*He runs a long thin line through the rest of the sentence, and contemplates
his work. Then he strikes out all the rest, too.*

DAVID: She came running toward him, her face scarlet in the
keen wind . . .

*He shakes his head and leans forward over his sheets of paper, and in
capital letters, in red ink, writes the following: SHE CAME RUNNING*

33

TOWARD HIM. Then he gives a sigh, shakes his head, runs a thick line through what he has written in capital letters and resolutely writes: "They met on the beach."
He turns round.
Karin is standing in the doorway.
DAVID: Hello, Kajsa dear. Awake already? It can't be more than four o'clock or so, can it?
KARIN: Hello, Daddy.
DAVID: Was there something you wanted?
Karin doesn't reply, but comes into the room. Closing the door behind her, she goes up to her father, sits down on his knee and throws her arm round his neck.
KARIN: Are you having trouble?
DAVID: Just putting the finishing touches to my book, you know, and that's never much fun.
KARIN: Read it to me.
DAVID: Later, when I've got the galleys. Why aren't *you* asleep?
KARIN: The birds. Just as the sun rose they gave such horrible cries. They woke me up and I was too frightened to go to sleep again.
DAVID: There, there. Everything will be all right now, you see.
He picks his daughter up and lays her in his own bed, spreads the coverlet over her, adjusts the pillow, passes his hand swiftly over her hair and cheek.
KARIN: Just like when I was little.
DAVID: You'll go to sleep now, you see.
He leaves her and sits down at his desk. Karin closes her eyes and yawns. The fierce tension leaves her face. She finds peace.
David observes his daughter—the pale face to which the sun has lent no color, the dark tangled hair, the deep blue shadows under her eyes.
Then he returns to his torments: the winding sentences, the hateful words, the situational banalities and the undimensional poverty of his characters.
DAVID: They met on the beach. It was high noon, with autumn in the air. It was high noon, with autumn in the air. It was high noon . . .
Minus's head appears at the window. His tousled hair is standing on end. Having slept well, he is gay and jolly.
MINUS: Daddy! Pst!
DAVID: Ssh. Karin's just dropped off.
MINUS: Martin asked me to bring up the nets. Coming?

DAVID: Coming.

He gets up quietly, puts on a short worn leather jacket and an old basque beret.

Impatiently, at the foot of the steps, Minus is waiting for him, passing the time by trying to do handstands, occasionally with some success.

MINUS: Last summer I found it as easy to walk on my hands as on my feet. Now I've grown so tall I can't keep my balance any more.

DAVID: Same thing with me.

MINUS: Ah. You mean spiritually. I understand.

Minus is proud of himself for understanding. Politely he stalks along beside his father.

DAVID: Are you writing anything yourself nowadays?

MINUS: Plays.

DAVID: May I read them?

MINUS: No, thanks. (*Pause*) Sorry. I didn't mean to hurt your feelings. But so far I think they're rotten.

DAVID: Have you written much?

MINUS: This summer I've put together thirteen three-acters and an opera.

DAVID: Whew!

MINUS: Yes, it pours out. The devil it does. Isn't it that way with you, too?

DAVID: No.

MINUS: What did you think of Karin's and my play, yesterday evening? Honestly.

DAVID: I couldn't see anything wrong with it.

MINUS: I thought it was shit.

Minus takes a jump and lands in the boat. Yawning, David follows him. Left alone, Karin—almost immediately—wakes up again. At first she lies still, briefly listening to David's and Minus's voices; then gets up and goes over to the writing desk.

She opens the right-hand drawer. A big black notebook, almost filled with her father's nervously pedantic handwriting, lies there. She sinks down on to the chair and reads slowly, carefully, whispering each word.

KARIN: "Her illness is hopeless, with occasional improvements. I have long suspected it, but the certainty, even so, is almost unbearable. To my horror, I note my own curiosity. The impulse to register its course, to note concisely her gradual dissolution. To make use of her."

She lets the book sink, lays it on the table, closes it, sits looking out of the window. Then she straightens her back, stuffs the book into its drawer and goes swiftly, silently, into her bedroom, where Martin, one hand under his cheek, is still sleeping.

Laughing, she falls over him and begins shaking him and pulling his hair.

KARIN: Wake up, Martin! How long are you going to sleep? The sun's high in the sky and you're going to be dipped. Martin, wake up!

MARTIN: Eh? What's the time?

KARIN: It's . . . well, it's nearly ten.

MARTIN: Oh my God, have I slept as late as that!

He sits up in bed and screws up his eyes sleepily, examines his wrist watch, shakes it and listens.

MARTIN: You wretch. It's only five.

KARIN: So what? Here have I been awake for ages and having all sorts of remarkable experiences—and you just sleep.

MARTIN: Come here, to me.

KARIN: No, up you get. We're going bathing. Daddy and Minus are out taking up the net.

Martin takes a firm grasp of Karin and pulls her to him into bed. She throws her arms around his neck and kisses him on the mouth. An impulsive embrace.

KARIN: The only thing wrong with you is, you sleep too much. And that, if I may say so, is why you're so sensible.

She laughs, and cries, and hugs him.

MARTIN: Karin, dearest. What is it?

KARIN: Nothing.

She presses her face against his arm, becomes tense and still.

MARTIN: What is it, Karin?

KARIN: There's something I've got to confess.

MARTIN: Well, out with it.

KARIN: Just now, when Daddy went out, I began poking about in his desk. I don't know what came over me, but I suddenly felt I had to.

MARTIN: Well?

KARIN: And I came across his diary.

MARTIN: Well?

KARIN: There was quite a lot in it.

MARTIN: About what?

KARIN: About me.

MARTIN: Oh, what had he written?

Karin presses her face even harder against Martin's arm. He becomes sick with fear. For a long while Karin doesn't say anything, then she shakes her head.

KARIN: I can't tell you.

MARTIN: About your illness?

KARIN (*nods silently*).

MARTIN: I told David you might possibly have a relapse. Perhaps he misunderstood me. No one can say your illness is incurable.

KARIN: Word of honour?

MARTIN (*nods*): Word of honour.

KARIN: There was something else, too.

MARTIN: Well?

KARIN: I can't tell you.

MARTIN: Please do.

KARIN (*shakes her head*): No, no, I can't. It's impossible.

MARTIN: Karin!

KARIN: You'll have to ask him yourself.

She throws herself on her back and laughs, but her eyes are full of terror; she stretches out her arms toward him. He bends over her and kisses her. She doesn't respond.

KARIN: Martin?

MARTIN: Yes.

KARIN: You must be patient with me. I'm sure I'll want you again, one day. Aren't you?

MARTIN: Of course. Naturally.

KARIN: Does it worry you?

MARTIN: Not in the least.

KARIN: I'm dreadfully tired, but anyway, let's get up and go and bathe. It isn't cold at all.

Martin sighs and smiles a wretched, put-on smile. Karin looks at him a moment, stands on the floor with one hand on her shoulder.

MARTIN: What?

KARIN: Think, Martin, to have a quiet woman, like a flower, who would give you children and coffee in bed. Who's big and warm and beautiful. Wouldn't it be lovely?

Martin takes a step toward Karin, but with a swift smile she eludes him.

MARTIN: It's you I love.

37

KARIN: Of course. But . . . even so.

MARTIN: I don't want anyone else.

Karin seems displeased with this answer and shakes her head. With a helpless gesture Martin offers her his hand.

KARIN: That's the odd thing about you. You always say the right words and do exactly the right things. But they're wrong, even so. Why's that?

Martin looks at her fixedly. His face is deeply tormented and troubled. But she won't respond to his appeal.

MARTIN: If I do the wrong thing, it's out of love. That's something you should know.

KARIN (*coldly*): Anyone who really loves always does the right thing by the person he loves.

MARTIN (*sadly*): Then you don't love me.

Long silence, then Karin puts out her hand and strokes Martin's cheek.

II

The day is warm and cloudy. It's blowing from the south and outside the sandbar white geese are riding the waves. Out at sea it is raining, grey-black curtains move forward across the horizon, and now and then a patch of sunlight flashes through the leaden light.

David and Martin are going into town to do some shopping. They are standing in the boat and have just started the motor. Karin is sitting on her haunches on the jetty and giving them their orders for the shopping. She and Martin go through the list a last time, underlining items and adding new ones.

DAVID: And just keep an eye on poor Minus, and see he doesn't go to sleep over his Latin.

KARIN: I've promised to hear his grammar.

DAVID: So long, then.

KARIN: 'Bye, Daddy.—Jesus, don't forget your cognac! And you can get some nice white wine, can't you?

DAVID: Exactly what I had in mind.

KARIN: 'Bye, darling! (*Kisses Martin*)

MARTIN: 'Bye. We'll be back for dinner.

Karin hands the painter to David and the boat heads out into the windy expanses of water. She gets up and stands awhile looking after them, swept by the warm wind.

Martin waves, and she waves eagerly back.

Thereafter, whistling quietly to herself, she goes off up toward the house, discovers a ladybird on the sleeve of her dress, takes it onto her forefinger, blows on it gently and makes it fly.

Minus is sitting in the garden's lilac alcove. Apparently deep in his studies, he chews a pen as he leans over the table.

Karin creeps up behind him, approaching soundlessly through the long grasses. Suddenly, when she is right behind his back, he notices her.

He gets a violent shock, shuts the magazine he has had spread out inside his Latin grammar, and flings it aside. Before Minus can grab it from her, Karin catches it. He stares furiously at his sister, starts to run off, but only manages a few yards, stopped by Karin's laughter.

MINUS: What the devil are you laughing at?

His hate-filled tone of voice makes Karin prick up her ears. At once she stops laughing, hands the magazine back to Minus, who, without looking at her, takes it and rolls it up.

MINUS: Well?

Karin doesn't reply. She sits down on the table. After pushing aside his exercise books, she scratches a midge bite on her knee.

MINUS: Why don't you say something?

He sulks a few moments, flings the magazine on the table in front of her and with a dramatic gesture points at it.

MINUS: Have a good look, if it amuses you.

She picks up the magazine and begins idly turning the pages, stops at a photo, turns the page, looks at the next one and the next.

KARIN: Which pictures do you think are so much fun, then?

MINUS *(grunts)*.

KARIN: Don't behave like a prudish old maid. Come on, show me.

Minus gives a short, joyless laugh, goes forward and stands beside Karin who is still sitting on the table. He turns the pages with a dirty thumb, points silently.

KARIN: You like that picture best?

MINUS *(nods)*.

KARIN: Why?

MINUS *(unhappily)*:   Because she's soft.

KARIN: I think she's terribly pretty, too.

Minus stares in despair at the picture and doesn't know where to turn, relieved, ashamed, red-handed, embarrassed and curious. Karin laughs.

KARIN: But she is a bit on the plump side, don't you think?

MINUS: And she's got long hair right down to . . . right down.
KARIN: She doesn't look as if she'd be much trouble.
MINUS; But that doesn't help at all!
Karin pretends not to hear this last explosion, just goes on turning the pages. Suddenly Minus seizes the magazine. She looks up. His face is twisted with rage and his posture as he leans forward is strange.
KARIN: Are you thinking of hitting me?
He spits in her face. Karin fixes him quietly and fearlessly with her eyes.
KARIN: Forgive me. It was my fault.
She takes hold of his hand and holds it firmly.
KARIN: Quiet, now, Minus. It's nothing dangerous. Nothing to worry about.
He tries to drag his hand away, but she won't let go.
KARIN: It was silly of me to be curious. Forgive me.
MINUS: I can't understand what flies into me. I don't want to, but suddenly it's happened.
Karin doesn't respond to this subject, but points toward his Latin grammar.
KARIN: Have you done your homework?
MINUS: A bit.
KARIN: Can I hear you?
MINUS: If you like. (*Pause*) I wonder if everyone is shut up in himself.
KARIN (*leafs through his grammar*): What d'you mean?
MINUS: Shut in. You in your affairs, me in mine. Each of us in his own box. All of us.
KARIN: I don't feel either shut in or lonely.
MINUS (*depressed*): Then I'm wrong, as usual.
They settle on the grass. Karin scratches her midge bite. The wind is warm and soft.
Minus runs his hand through his close-cropped hair.
A long while they struggle dutifully with Latin grammar. Present and imperfect, conjunctive, subordinate clauses governed by a verb in the future simple in certain indicative subordinate clauses. The referant conjunctive has replaced the indicative to show that the clause constitutes a statement, an opinion or a thought. Affirmo me facturum est ut possim —I assure you I will do my best.
Both yawn, help each other, struggle, turn back, look into the book together, shake their heads, yawn, lie down on their backs on the grass, sit up again. Nothing is any good. Time passes very slowly and the cloudy summer's day is mild and soft around them. If one conjunctive subordinate clause

depends on another, the conjunctive present governs a main tense sequence in the main subordinate clause, while the other tenses of the conjunctive govern a historic tense sequence.

KARIN: It's terribly warm.

MINUS: I've been up since four-thirty.

KARIN: Let's have a cigarette. Got any?

Minus digs into his pocket and fishes out a packet, in which only one solitary, rather crumpled cigarette is left. He breaks it in two, offers one half to Karin. They light up and smoke in silence, sitting face to face, tailorwise. Silence.

KARIN: Minus.

MINUS: H'm?

KARIN: If you look for a long time, with your head bent back or turned to one side, it can become rather horrible, I tell you.

MINUS: Horrible?

KARIN: Yet exciting. You won't tell Daddy or Martin about it, will you? They don't understand, particularly not Martin. He's so weak and anxious and has enough of his own troubles. No, they don't understand. They'd just think I was ill. Do you think so, too?

MINUS: That you're ill? No. No, I don't believe it.

KARIN: I thought not. Because you're stronger. Over and over again I've been meaning to tell you about this new thing. It's like a . . .

She checks herself, stares silently and darkly at Minus, who meets her gaze with complete calm.

MINUS: You can rely on me.

KARIN: It's so hard, not being able to talk about something you're thinking of every moment. I'm sure I can tell you. *The Others* wouldn't mind.

MINUS: The Others?

KARIN: Look, Minus, you mustn't pester me with idiotic questions. I'll tell you as much as I dare. Otherwise we'd better stop at once.

MINUS: I was only curious.

KARIN: That's all right. I don't mind *you* being curious.

She reflects awhile, takes a last deep tug at her cigarette, scrapes a little hole with her finger in the sand and buries the stub.

KARIN: Coming? I'll show you something.

41

She goes softly ahead through the garden, into the house and up the stairs to the first floor. She opens the door to the room with the wallpaper.
Silent, tense, Minus follows her. She closes the door behind him, goes up to the wall and strokes her hand over the wallpaper.

KARIN: D'you know what—I can walk straight through this wall.

MINUS (*doesn't reply*).

KARIN: Can't imagine how it's done. Early this morning I was woken by a voice calling me, quite definitely calling. I got up and came to this room. Just at sunrise, and inside me a tremendous longing, a tremendous power. One day someone called to me from behind the wallpaper, and I looked inside the cupboard, but it was empty. The voice went on calling me, so I pressed myself against the wall and it opened up like a lot of leaves *and there I was inside*!

Breaking off, she smiles quickly and mockingly.

MINUS: What is it?

KARIN: You think I'm making it up?

MINUS (*shakes his head*).

Again she runs her hand over the wallpaper, seems suddenly absent. Minus is very tense, but doesn't dare disturb the sudden silence.

KARIN: I come into a big room, quite still and silent, people are moving about and someone speaks to me and I understand. It's so lovely, I feel so safe. Some of the faces are radiant with light.

All are waiting for him who is to come, but no one worries. They say I can be with them when it happens.

MINUS: Why are you crying?

KARIN: No, it's nothing, nothing dangerous. But you see, Minus, sometimes I'm overcome with such a terrible longing. I long for that moment when the door will open and all faces are turned toward him who's to come.

MINUS: Who is it, who's coming?

KARIN: I don't know, no one has said anything definite, but I believe God is going to reveal himself to us. And he'll come in to us through that door. (*Pause*) Everyone's so calm—and so gentle. And they're waiting. And their love . . . LOVE . . .

She checks herself and quietly repeats the word, several times over. Then she begins speaking again, but in a changed, low voice.

KARIN: I'm strong and I can bear my guilt.

42

MINUS: Have you done something wrong?

KARIN: Yes, I have. (*Pause*) I turn away from Martin. He stands there calling me, but I can't help him. It's just a game.

MINUS: Doesn't he notice anything?

KARIN: I can't say for sure. But I must choose between him and the other thing. And I've decided. I've given up Martin.

Karin is now very far away, but at the same time stern and clear, as if a voice foreign to her own self were speaking through her mouth.

MINUS (*frightened*): Is all that real?

Her face turns pale in an expression of sharp pain, she shakes her head.

KARIN: I'm standing in the middle, between them; and sometimes I'm not sure. I know I've been ill, been under treatment. But my illness was like dreams, and this isn't dreams, it's real. *It must be real!*

MINUS: For me it isn't real. Not a scrap.

She doesn't reply, just stands still and passes her hand over the wallpaper's patterns and patches. Her gaze is lost on the horizon out to sea.

MINUS (*in a low voice*): For me it isn't real.

KARIN: Yes. A god comes down from the mountain. He goes through the dark forest. Everywhere in the twilight, in the silence, are wild beasts. *That* must be reality. After all I'm not dreaming, and I'm telling the truth. Sometimes I'm in one world, sometimes in the other, and I can't do a thing about it. Though of course I know I'm doing wrong, both to you and to Martin.

MINUS: What about Daddy, then? Why not to him?

KARIN: I don't know. Can't explain.

MINUS: Why not?

KARIN: Because then you'd hate him and I don't want that. Poor Daddy, with his jealousy. You must be nice to Daddy, Minus. It'll be hardest for him.

Minus observes his sister, but she appears sunk in her own thoughts.

MINUS (*quietly*): Shall we go and bathe?

KARIN (*doesn't reply*).

MINUS: Then I'll go by myself.

KARIN (*doesn't reply*).

Minus gets up and with bowed head goes to the door.

KARIN: I'm sleepy. I'm going to have a little sleep. Shut the door when you go.

He turns round. Karin has lain down on the floor. She is lying on her side with her right hand high up between her legs and her head pressed downward. Minus takes a step toward her.

KARIN: No, leave me in peace. Go away. I want to sleep. Go away. I'm tired. Go away.

Minus goes slowly to the door. Karin lies motionless. He stops again and looks at her, tense, suspicious. Then he goes out, closing the door behind him, and stands a few moments listening.

MINUS: What the hell am I to do?

Quickly he runs downstairs. Rushes up again, flings the door open and meets Karin face to face.

KARIN: Well, have you done your Latin properly, eh?

MINUS (*nods*).

KARIN: Come along, then. We'll go down and get on with it.

MINUS (*nods, swallows*).

KARIN: Though I think we must have some tea first.

She precedes him down the stairs. On the lowest step she turns and looks sternly at Minus.

KARIN: Are you going to tell Daddy and Martin?

MINUS: Tell them what?

KARIN: Cunning. But you can't fool me. This evening you'll take Martin aside and say I've got to talk to you about Karin. And then you'll spill the beans.

MINUS: Can't you tell him yourself?

KARIN: Promise me not to tell.

MINUS: I promise.

KARIN: You're the only one who understands. But say the least word to anyone, and you've deceived me.

They go through the hall into the kitchen.

David and Martin have run the boat ashore in the lee of a creek and taken out their lunch basket. Martin, who has finished eating, is throwing pebbles in the water. David is drinking coffee out of the Thermos cup. Neither says a word.

DAVID: What's up?

MARTIN: What d'you mean?

DAVID: You don't say anything. You seem almost hostile.

MARTIN: Maybe there's no point in talking to you about it. I don't know.

DAVID: Please do.

MARTIN: It's about Karin.

DAVID: Karin. Well?

MARTIN: She's been poking around in your desk and came across your diary. Of course she read . . .

DAVID: No. (*Pause*) Oh my God.

Suddenly terrified he lifts his hand to his face.

MARTIN: What did you write?

DAVID: Oh my God!

MARTIN: Karin wanted me to ask you.

DAVID: I wrote that her illness is hopeless. I also wrote that I feel a terrible impulse to observe its development.

Martin stares at David. His face is twisted with disgust. David has crumpled, passes one hand across his knee, over and over again.

DAVID: I haven't any excuse. Can't defend myself.

MARTIN: It's always 'you' and 'yours'.

DAVID (*shakes his head*).

MARTIN: You're absolutely perverted in your frigid lack of feeling. 'Observe its development'. That's significant.

DAVID (*takes a deep breath*): You don't understand.

MARTIN: No, I certainly don't. But one thing I do understand: you're chasing subjects. Your daughter's illness. Bloody hell, what a fine idea!

DAVID (*quietly*): I love her, Martin.

MARTIN: You—love! In your emptiness there's no room for feelings, and as for any sense of decency, you just haven't got it. You know how everything should be expressed. At every moment you have the right word. There's only *one* phenomenon you haven't an inkling of: life itself.

DAVID (*looks at Martin*).

MARTIN: You're cowardly and sloppy, but on one point you're almost a genius. At explaining things away and apologizing.

DAVID: What d'you want me to do?

MARTIN: Write your book! Maybe it'll give you what you long for more than anything else: a name as an author. Then your daughter won't have been sacrificed in vain. I can . . . I should . . .

He checks himself and bites his lip. David looks at him. David's face has fallen in, his hand still goes on moving restlessly to and fro over his knee.

DAVID: No. Say what you're thinking.

MARTIN: You've got a god you flirt with in your novels, but I can tell you, both your faith and your doubt are equally

45

unconvincing. What strikes one most is your monstrous inventiveness.

DAVID: Don't you think I know?

MARTIN: Well, then. Why go on? Why don't you do something respectable for a living?

DAVID: What could I do?

MARTIN: Have you ever written so much as a true word in any of your books? Reply if you can.

DAVID: I don't know.

MARTIN: There! But the worst of it is your lies are so refined they resemble truth.

DAVID: I do my best.

MARTIN: Maybe. *But you never succeed.*

DAVID: I know.

MARTIN: You're empty and clever and now you think you'll fill your emptiness with Karin's extinction. The only thing I don't understand is how you fancy you can mix God up in all this. He must be more inscrutable than ever.

DAVID: Martin, there's just one thing I want to ask you.

MARTIN: Go ahead.

DAVID: Can you always control your innermost thoughts?

MARTIN: I'm not so complicated, thank God. My world's very simple. But rather clear and human.

DAVID: Even so, you've several times wished Karin was dead.

MARTIN: No. Absolutely not! Nobody but you would hit on such an idea.

DAVID: Can you swear to me you've never thought such a thought? After all, it would be quite logical. You know her illness is hopeless and you know from your convictions there's no sense in your sufferings. In which case she might as well be dead.

MARTIN: You're grotesque.

DAVID: Depends entirely on the point of view.

David lights his pipe, his hand trembles but otherwise he seems completely calm.

MARTIN: This is a meaningless discussion.

DAVID (*grimly*): Not quite.

MARTIN: I love her and I'm helpless. I can only stand at her side and watch her being transformed into a wretched tormented animal. Already I see I can't reach her, how she turns away from me. Sometimes it's almost as if she hated me.

DAVID: The main thing is to believe in one's own good intentions. Then everything solves itself, as if by magic. Provided you go through the correct motions. Activity stimulates self-confidence and hinders reflection.

MARTIN: Are you speaking of me?

DAVID: Shouldn't dare. I'm talking in general principles. I assure you my irony is mostly directed against myself.

MARTIN: But you can find consolation in your religion.

DAVID: Yes.

MARTIN: And inscrutable grace.

DAVID: Yes.

MARTIN: It *is* inscrutable?

David raises his hand and looks out across the wind-blown sea outside the creek, with its scents of pine forest and algae. His hand still trembles and his pipe has gone out.

DAVID: I'll tell you something. Down there in Switzerland I decided to kill myself. I'd hired a small car and found a precipice. As I drove out there I was quite calm. It was a very lonely road, no traffic. And it was evening; down in the valley it was already dark. I was empty, without fear, remorse or expectation. So I went straight for the precipice. As I pressed the accelerator down, the engine stalled; the gear stopped me dead. The car slid a few yards on the loose gravel surface, then hung there with its front wheels over the edge. I dragged myself out, trembling all over; had to sit down under the cliff on the other side of the road. And there I sat, gasping for breath, for several hours.

MARTIN: What are you telling me all this for?

DAVID: I want to tell you I no longer have any façades to keep up. Truth requires no catastrophes. I can see myself.

He knocks out his pipe and blows in it. Martin leans forward, gnawed by acute anxiety.

MARTIN: This hasn't anything to do with Karin.

DAVID: Yes, I think it has.

MARTIN: I don't understand.

DAVID: Out of my emptiness something was born which I hardly dare touch or give a name to. A love. (*Pause*) For Karin and Minus. And you.

47

For a long time they sit silent, motionless. David quickly puts his hand on Martin's and, just as quickly, withdraws it. It is a shy but unambiguous gesture of friendship.

DAVID: Maybe I'll tell you, one day. I don't dare to now. But if . . . I mean if it is as I . . . Let's leave it at that for the time being.

He gives a dry laugh. Martin gets up and begins punting the boat out of the creek. David starts up the motor.

During the rest of their trip they hardly speak. In the evening they run into heavy rain.

Minus and Karin have sat down at the far end of the old jetty. He is busy painting an old rocking chair and she is cleaning fish for dinner. Now and then Minus whistles a fragment of a tune but immediately remembers his depression and falls silent.

Karin gets up and passses the back of her hand over her hair.

KARIN: Here comes the rain.

Minus checks himself and reaches out his hand, but immediately withdraws it.

MINUS: No it doesn't!

But Karin stands looking out over the sea.

KARIN: Yes, here comes the rain.

Minus follows the direction of her gaze.

The sea is grey, almost still. The clouds hang heavy over the line of the horizon. Every sound is hushed.

MINUS: I don't think we'll be getting it.

After putting the cleaned fish on an earthenware dish, Karin folds up the newspaper with the remains. Then she takes off her apron.

KARIN: Yes, here comes the rain.

She makes a pained grimace, and with the same nervous gesture runs her hand over her hair again. She goes up toward the house, stops a moment, turns round, but at once goes on again. Minus, suddenly overcome by anxiety, looks out across the sea.

A bird screeches above his head. It, too, sounds anxious. He looks to see where the sound came from. It is repeated again and again, frightening and demanding. A black squall is coming in across the water, which splashes and clucks beneath the jetty. Minus shivers in the summer heat.

His fear is too much for him. He runs up toward the house, into the garden, calls for Karin. No reply.

He goes into the house. Looks and calls. But Karin has vanished.

Now he's up in the room with the wallpaper. The wardrobe door. Empty, silent.
Now and then the seabird's cry, anxious, demanding.
Minus runs downstairs and stops irresolutely in the hall. The door to the kitchen is ajar, the curtain flutters in a sudden draft. The sea has begun to get up, rolling and mumbling.
He rushes out of the house, through the garden, down to the shore, whose line he follows.
At length, out of breath, he stops near the old wreck.
It's an old timber schooner, with broken mast and shattered bows. Its hold gapes black and open. Rotten tackle and ropes hang from its rail and deck-timbers. The sternhouse with its shattered windows and collapsed roof rests against the vertical stump of a mast. The hull lies on a grass-grown sandy spit running out a few yards into the water.
On the top of the spit of sand stands a sea-mark.
Minus clambers up onto the wreck and stands there a moment, listening. Then he creeps cautiously forward to the hold, peering down into the darkness; but can distinguish nothing. So he climbs down into the hold.
The hull has great cracks in its sides, here and there daylight filters in and there's also a faint daylight from the hatch. In the bows the waves sweep in and out, but in the stern the deck is firm and undamaged.
When Minus's eyes have got used to the dark, he discovers a figure, further in, and he hears breathing.
MINUS: Karin!
(No answer.)
MINUS: Karin! Is it you?
He sees her reaching a hand out to him, and he goes closer. She is lying hunched up in a corner like an animal, her face dirty, her skirt pulled up over her stomach. Minus falls on his knees close beside her and tries to catch her eye.
MINUS: It's me, Karin.
Without replying, Karin presses her face against his. Her eyes are closed, her breathing is hot and febrile.
Suddenly she has clasped him tight and he falls headlong on top of her, struggles to get free, but can't, sinks more deeply into her. He catches a glimpse of naked skin, an odour of seaweed, rotten wood, the sea bottom. She holds him tight to her with her arms and legs, but her face is averted, her mouth tightly closed.
Then the rain begins thudding on the deck. Slowly, he frees himself and lifts his head. He sits beside her, incapable of movement, choked by tears.

49

The rain drums ever harder, pouring in through the open hatch of the hold. It's cold and damp, down there in the darkness.

MINUS: We must go home.

Karin doesn't reply, hardly notices him. Minus throws himself at her, begins to yell, shouting her name, shaking her.

Slowly she comes back to consciousness, sinks down with her arms between her legs. Her pale face expresses only a vast anxiety.

KARIN: You must help me, I'm ill.

MINUS: Come along, we'll go home.

KARIN: I can't leave. I must stay here.

MINUS: What shall we do?

KARIN: You must help me.

MINUS: Can't you tell me how to help you?

KARIN: You must help me.

Minus grasps her wrists to raise her up but, terrified, she resists with all her strength.

KARIN: No. I can't leave. I'm so thirsty.

MINUS: Shall I get you some water?

Karin seems absent again. Minus gets up and, in an obscure blend of terror and desire to help his sister, clambers up through the hatch to the deck and runs off toward the house.

Karin creeps on all fours toward the water in the bows, sinks her face in it, and drinks long and deep. Then she drags herself back to her corner, where she crouches, shivering.

Minus rushes into his room and throws himself on his knees on the floor and clasps his hands, bends his head and presses his hands to his lips.

MINUS (*whispering*): God . . . God . . . help us!

Like a cry and a whisper, the rain beats in fierce gusts against the window-pane, blurring all outlines. The room's interior is in semi-darkness and the wind presses against the old house, which sighs and creaks.

Again and again he calls on God. At length, exhausted, he falls silent. Stands still a few moments, then tears a couple of blankets off his bed and goes out into the hall, where he rolls them up in a raincoat. Then he flings on his oilskins and hurries back toward the wreck.

Karin is on all fours beneath the hatch, rocking to and fro, feeling very sick; opens her mouth convulsively, as if yawning; now and then a whimpering sound forces itself out of her throat.

Minus jumps down into the hold and taking out the blankets from beneath his raincoat unfolds them. He manages to move Karin out of the rain and covers her as best he can. Sits down against the ship's side with his back

50

*to a great beam, and draws her to him. Then holds her in his arms. This
seems to quieten her, the whimpering ceases and she sinks into a twilit,
semi-comatose absence.*

*Slowly the rain ceases, the squalls desist, only a few drops of rain drip
from the edges of the hold as little rivulets run down toward the water in
the bows. Again a little while and the evening sun breaks through as the
cloud banks draw off. In the interior of the wreck shafts of light crisscross
the darkness.*

*Minus is sitting somewhere in eternity with his sick sister in his arms.
He is empty, exhausted, frozen. Reality, as he has known it until now, has
been shattered, ceased to exist. Neither in his dreams nor his fantasies has
he known anything to correspond to this moment of weightlessness and
grief. His mind has forced its way through the membrane of merciful
ignorance. From this moment on his senses will change and harden, his
receptivity will become sharpened, as he goes from the make-believe
world of innocence to the torment of insight. The world of contingency and
chance has been transformed into a universe of law.*

*Now the motorboat can be heard out at sea. Minus carefully disentangles
himself and lays his raincoat over Karin. He hurries off to meet David and
Martin.*

*A few words explain the situation. They half-walk, half-run toward the
wreck. Martin and David climb aboard first, Minus follows slowly.*

*Martin falls on his knee in front of Karin and gently raises her head.
She looks at him a long while, moves her dry lips. At last she can form
words.*

KARIN: What's the time?

MARTIN: Five, I think.

KARIN: I've been dreadfully ill, but I feel better now. Poor
Minus!

*She frees herself carefully from Martin and gets up, her eyes seek her
father, who is standing a little way off. She goes up to the bows, and
squatting there rinses her face; the palms of her hands rest on the surface
of the water.*

KARIN: I want to talk to Daddy, alone.

MARTIN: Can't we go home first?

KARIN: I don't know how long I'll be calm. And I must talk to
Daddy before it comes on again.

MARTIN: Karin, darling! Darling Karin!

KARIN *(tormented)*: It won't be long. Please.

Martin gets up slowly, passes close to David.

51

MARTIN: I'll go to the farm and ring for the ambulance.

DAVID (*nods silently*).

Martin clambers out of the hold. Minus stands in front of him shivering in the bright sunshine.

MARTIN: You know where my medicine bag is. Run and fetch it, will you? In a while we'll have to give her a shot. Or we won't get her away.

Without a word Minus turns and runs up to the house. Martin goes off into the wood, toward the farm.

David has sat down a few feet away from Karin. She is still leaning over the glimmering, trembling water, which mirrors bright reflections of light on to the dark and rough timbers of the hulk.

KARIN: What's the time?

DAVID: Just past five.

KARIN: It was raining dreadfully just now, wasn't it?

DAVID: Yes. Dreadfully.

Karin sighs and gets up, stretches herself, reaches up her hand to the edge of the hold and screws up her eyes in the strong sunlight.

KARIN: It's so hard to breathe. Like when you've been crying for ages.—Daddy?

DAVID: Yes?

KARIN: I want to stay in the hospital now! I don't want any more treatments. D'you think they'll let me off? If you're firm about it?

DAVID: I don't know.

KARIN: Nobody can live in two worlds. You have to choose. It's more than I can stand, going back and forth between one and the other. I simply can't stand it.

She goes up toward the stern and sits down in the half-light; a shaft of sunlight cuts close to her face, illumining it as she leans forward.

Arms round her knees, she rests her chin on them.

KARIN: It couldn't go on.

DAVID: What?

KARIN: The hatred.

DAVID: What hatred?

KARIN: I didn't do it because I wanted to. It was a voice told me what to do.

DAVID: The voice that told you to look in my diary.

KARIN (*nods*).

DAVID: And then go to Martin and tell him what you'd read.

52

KARIN (*nods*): Though I didn't want to.

DAVID: No, I don't think you did.

KARIN: I've done something worse than that. Much worse.

Suddenly she begins to cry, silently and hopelessly.

DAVID: You must tell me.

KARIN: I struggled against it, but I couldn't escape.

DAVID: When did it happen?

KARIN: Now. Poor little Minus.

She bites her lip to hold back her tears, but they fill her eyes.

DAVID: I'll talk to him.

KARIN: I can't understand it. No, I can't understand.

DAVID: Try to be calm, Karin.

KARIN: And then the room, with all those people waiting.

DAVID: Yes?

KARIN: The bright ones who wait until the door opens and God comes to them. They say I can be there then, too. But then the voices come and I have to do what the voice says. I can't make any sense of it. Is it because I'm ill? Daddy, it's so dreadful, realizing how muddled I am and not being able to understand it. Last time. . . And now again. Yet it isn't really anything terrible, either. I remember what it was like for all those other poor wretches who'd got the same illness as me. All the horrible things they told me. And how they screamed and threw themselves on the ground, and hurt themselves till they were covered in blood.

She sits silent for a while.

DAVID: I want to ask you to forgive me, Karin.

KARIN (*doesn't reply*).

DAVID: I've always had a guilty conscience toward you and I've hardened my heart and turned away.

KARIN: You didn't want to be disturbed.

DAVID: When I think of all the lives I've sacrificed to my so-called art, it makes me sick.

KARIN: You mean Mummy?

DAVID: When Mummy got ill I went away and left you with Granny. After all, I had my novel to think of. When Mummy died I had my big success, and it meant so much more to me than her death I was even secretly glad—yet I loved your mother in my own confused, selfish way. Oh, Karin, how one's eyes burn when one sees oneself.

53

David passes his hands over his eyes and looks at the glittering blinding light from the water.

KARIN: And when I got ill you went to Switzerland, didn't you?

DAVID: I couldn't bear it, your inheriting Mummy's illness. So I fled headlong. After all, I had to finish my book.

KARIN: Will it be a good one?

David doesn't answer. He shakes his head. He puts out his hand to Karin, and she grips it. Both are absorbed in a deep feeling of unconditionally belonging together.

DAVID: It's like this. One draws a magic circle around oneself, shutting out everything that hasn't any place in one's own private little game. Every time life smashes the circle the game turns into something grey, tiny, ridiculous. So one draws a new circle, builds up new barriers.

KARIN: Poor little Daddy.

DAVID: Yes. Poor little Daddy, who's forced to live in reality.

Karin gets up; she is very tired, has difficulty in standing steadily, and supports herself with one hand against the bulkhead.

KARIN: Let's go home now, before it comes on again. Martin's rung for the ambulance, hasn't he? I've got to pack.

David draws his daughter to him, holding her fast in a silent pathetic embrace.

Then they climb out of the hold.

As they come into view Minus turns and rushes up toward the wood. Karin calls after him. For a moment he looks back, but dashes on, stumbles, and disappears among the bare dead trees.

KARIN (*quietly*): How soon will the ambulance be here?

MARTIN: In an hour or so.

KARIN: I'll just change and pack.

Martin is standing there with his little brown doctor's bag at his feet. He picks it up, as if caught red-handed.

KARIN: What have you fetched your bag for?

MARTIN: Maybe you could do with a sedative.

KARIN: I'm quite calm.

To come close to her and support her he makes to put his arm round her shoulder; but she gently disengages herself.

KARIN: No thanks, I can manage.

They begin walking toward the house: Karin and Martin side by side, David a few steps behind. The evening sun burns hotly over the sea and the white sand. The light is fierce, almost unreal.

KARIN: The light's so strong.

Martin turns round and looks out over the sea gleaming in the path of the sun. To north and east there are still black cloud-masses.

KARIN: Daddy, you must help Minus with his Latin.

DAVID: I've thought of that.

Martin's features, drawn with grief and flushed with agitation, are a rather preposterous red hue. Behind the thick glasses his glance seems half dead.

MARTIN: Mustn't forget to take my keys into town. The janitor's probably away on holiday.

KARIN: Aren't you coming back, then?

MARTIN: No, I'm staying. It's better that way.

They have reached the house and are walking through the garden.

KARIN: What a shame. Now we won't be able to go mushroom-picking together.

Karin halts by the summerhouse and picks up something in the grass. It is the silver-paper crown she had worn when playing the princess in Minus' theatricals. Wet with the rain, it immediately falls to pieces. She throws it away, and goes on down the path through the currant bushes.

KARIN: Help me pack, will you, Martin? I'm so dreadfully tired.

Martin follows her into the bedroom. They talk in low tones.

David remains briefly on the steps. It is a still, hot summer's evening, with mild airs blowing in from the sea. The garden is swarming with life and heady with strong scents after the rain. A glimpse of Minus in the distance among the trees.

DAVID: Come along, Minus. Let's have a chat.

But without replying Minus, like a shy animal, vanishes swiftly into the foliage.

David beckons to him again, several times, in vain.

He goes into his room.

On his writing desk lies the manuscript of his novel. He picks it up and weighs it in his hands. Then he lights a fire in the stove.

Methodically, he feeds bundle ujter bundle of the typewritten sheets into the flames.

III

The suitcases are lying open on the bed. Karin has already changed for her journey. Martin is searching for a clean shirt in the chest of drawers.

KARIN: Your shirts are washed but not ironed.

MARTIN: Then I'll have to travel in this one. Anyway I've got other shirts in town.

KARIN: Help me shut my case, will you?

They do it together, struggling with the lock.

MARTIN: It's my shoes. I can leave them here.

He takes out a pair of shoes and puts them on the floor. Troubled, Karin looks at them.

KARIN: Can't you put them on? And leave the ones you're wearing?

MARTIN: They've got to go to the shoemaker's.

KARIN: Have you an aspirin?

Martin looks round for one. Karin massages her forehead with her forefinger.

MARTIN: I thought I put the brown suitcase here.

KARIN: You left it in the kitchen.

Martin remembers, goes out to the kitchen.

Quite right. His suitcase is lying on the kitchen table. He gets out some aspirin and fills a glass of water with a dipper from a bucket.

Then he goes back to the bedroom. Karin has vanished.

At once Martin runs out to the porch, looking in every direction. But Karin is nowhere to be seen. He flings open the door to David's room.

MARTIN: Have you seen Karin?

David shakes his head, and Martin instantly leaves again. David goes to the door and looks out into the hall. Then hurries upstairs to the upper floor. At once he hears Karin's voice from the depths of the room to his left.

He goes nearer. Through the door, which is ajar, he sees Karin standing in the room with her face turned to the right and speaking to some invisible person, apparently much larger than herself. Her words are scarcely audible.

Hearing footsteps, he turns. Martin is coming toward him. In his hand, as if it were his last resource, he holds his brown doctor's bag. He stops behind David and looks into the room. Karin continues her secretive conversation.

KARIN: I know it won't be long now. It's so good to know that. But our waiting has been only a joy to us.

Martin tries to catch David's glance, but he steps to one side; immediately Martin is on the move.

KARIN: Martin, tread softly!

MARTIN: Yes, yes.

KARIN: They say he is coming any moment now. That we must be ready.

MARTIN: Karin!

KARIN: Yes?

MARTIN: We were going into town, have you forgotten?

KARIN: I can't go now, surely you understand that!

MARTIN: You're wrong, Karin. Nothing is happening in there. (*Pause*) Karin! No god is going to come out of that door.

KARIN: They've said he's coming any moment now, and I must be here.

MARTIN: Karin, dear. It simply isn't so.

KARIN: You mustn't talk so loud. If you can't be quiet you'd better go away.

She turns her face toward Martin.

Suddenly she is furiously upset.

MARTIN: Karin, dear, come along with me now.

KARIN (*suddenly appealing*): Why've you got to spoil it? Go away, let me be alone, just this moment.

Suddenly Martin feels very tired. He takes a few steps backwards and sinks down in the only chair in the room, removes his glasses and wipes them with his handkerchief.

Karin, her gaze fixed steadily on the wallpapered door, clasps her hands and falls on her knees. Her face is completely calm, almost radiant.

KARIN (*in a low voice*): They say he's in the next room and they can hear his voice. (*Even lower*) Martin, dearest, forgive me for being so nasty just now. But can't you kneel down too, and clasp your hands, here, beside me? It looks so demonstrative and odd, you sitting there in that chair. I know you don't believe; but for my sake, Martin.

Martin shakes his head. He tries to say something but he can't. In the end he slips down on to the floor beside his wife and leans his head against her shoulder.

MARTIN: Karin, dearest, dearest, dearest.

Gently, as if disturbed and hurt by his sudden and as it were indecent intervention, she draws away. He reaches out his hand, but she doesn't take it.

Now the engines of the helicopter can be heard, the sound grows swiftly until within a few moments it is a tremendous roar, shaking the whole house. As the machine passes close above the roof there is a brief glimpse of it through the window, a gigantic dark insect.

57

The windowpanes rattle and Karin slowly gets up. The door in the wall-paper opens wide against the darkness of the cupboard.
She stands tense, radiant with expectancy. Then her countenance changes. She seems to see something coming out of the cupboard, something that swiftly approaches her. Shrinks away. Runs several steps backwards. Flattens herself against the wall. Presses her hands between her legs. A gurgling scream of horror forces itself out of her throat. With all her force she flings herself at Martin, who falls over and loses his glasses. As she clings to him the animal-like cry forces itself again and again out of her mouth.
Martin has grasped hold of her, but she tears herself away. Rushing out of the door, she meets David. He, too, tries to catch her. But she is suddenly endowed with immense, superhuman strength.
Rushing for the stairs, she takes a couple of steps down but stops.
At the bottom stands Minus, looking up at her. She sinks down on the step and arches herself backwards, all the time making as if to protect herself with her hands. David throws himself down beside her, clasps her tight.
The next moment Martin arrives. In his right hand he has his hypodermic needle.
MARTIN: Hold her legs.
This in a suddenly calm tone to Minus, who obeys, flinging himself over the violently kicking feet.
Martin draws aside her skirt, rubs the outside of her thigh with a wad of cotton, inserts his needle.
Karin flings herself about in convulsive jerks. Martin protects her head with both his hands. David, mumbling inaudible words, embraces her. Gradually the attack subsides and she becomes still.
Martin fetches water in a cup. She drinks thirstily. Then sits up and pulls her skirt down over her knees, straightening her hair.
KARIN: I was frightened.
A few moments she is silent, takes the cup from Martin and swallows another gulp.
KARIN: The door opened. But the god who came out was a spider. He had six legs and moved very fast across the floor.
She is shaken by terror and disgust as she speaks. By an effort of will she controls herself.
KARIN: He came up to me and I saw his face, a loathsome, evil face. And he clambered up onto me and tried to force himself into me. But I protected myself. All the time I saw

his eyes. They were cold and calm. When he couldn't force himself into me, he climbed quickly up onto my breast and my face and went on up the wall.

Again she is silent. Martin takes the cup from her hand and unscrews his hypodermic needle. She meets Minus' gaze, but no longer recognizes him.

KARIN: I've seen God.

This she says with complete calm, but beneath the surface trembles a new and boundless horror whose swiftly growing roots are entangling themselves around her soul.

Now voices are heard out in the yard. Someone knocks at the door. David goes out. After a few moments he is back in the hall.

DAVID: They're waiting at the jetty.

Cautiously, Martin touches Karin's arm. She scarcely reacts. Then Minus takes her by the hand and leads her into her bedroom, helps her on with her coat, combs her hair and holds out her handbag to her. She opens it, takes out her sunglasses, puts them on.

David leads her gently out of the door and down towards the jetty. She follows obediently, in complete apathy. Now and then she gives a faint moan.

Minus is left standing in the hall. Silent, tearless, he sits down with his back to the rusty iron stove and sobs.

Hearing the engines starting up, he rushes out on to the slope in front of the house. The aircraft lifts. Almost immediately it is swallowed up in the mist and the fierce sunshine.

Far off, down on the shore, David's body throws a long shadow on the sand's whiteness. Minus runs across the garden to its deepest corner into the merciful shade of the summerhouse.

David has gone down to the nets. Examines them closely as he fills his pipe. Puts it into his mouth, but doesn't light it. Again and again he screws up his eyes, looking into the jagged evening light, as if to burn away every tear of self-pity.

When at length he turns round Minus is standing behind him.

MINUS: Daddy, I'm scared.

For a moment David raises one arm as if to embrace the boy but when Minus makes a slight evasive movement checks himself.

MINUS: As I was sitting in the wreck down there, holding Karin, reality burst in pieces for me. D'you understand what I mean?

DAVID: I understand.

MINUS: Reality burst and I fell out. It's like in a dream, though real. Anything can happen—*anything*, Daddy!

DAVID: Yes, I know.

MINUS: I'm so terrified I could scream.

DAVID: Come.

He touches Minus' hand. Together they begin walking along the beach, the hard sunshine on their faces. They walk in silence, side by side. Then David puts his arm round Minus' shoulders. They follow the shoreline. Minus is barefooted and now and then the water laps his feet.

MINUS: I can't live with this new thing, Daddy.

DAVID: Yes, you can. But you must have something to hold on to.

MINUS: And what could that be? A god? A spider god like Karin's? Or an invisible potentate somewhere in the dark? No. It's no good.

Silence.

MINUS: No, Daddy, it's no good. God doesn't exist in my world.

Silence. They follow the shoreline further.

MINUS (*full of anxiety*): Give me some proof of God.

Silence.

MINUS: You can't.

DAVID: Yes, I can. But you must listen carefully to what I'm saying, Minus.

MINUS: That's just what I need, to listen.

DAVID: It's written: *God is love.*

MINUS: For me that's just words and nonsense.

DAVID: Wait a moment and don't interrupt.

They have walked out on to a low sandy spit, almost invisible, submerged in the water. It seems as if they were standing in the midst of the sea's whiteness, with the whiteness of the summer sky above their heads, as if they were shut in beneath a globe of milky glass. Infinitely tiny in this silent misty whiteness.

DAVID: I only want to give you an indication of where my own hopes lie.

MINUS: And that's in God's love?

DAVID: In the knowledge that love exists as something real in the world of men.

MINUS: Of course it's a special sort of love you're referring to.

DAVID: *Every* sort of love, Minus! The highest and the lowest, the poorest and the richest, the most ridiculous and the most sublime. The obsessive and the banal. All sorts of love.

60

MINUS (*silent*): Longing for love.

DAVID: Longing and denial. Disbelieving and being consoled.

MINUS: So love is the proof?

DAVID: We can't know whether love proves God's existence or whether love is itself God. After all, it doesn't make very much difference.

MINUS: For you God and love are one and the same phenomenon.

DAVID: I let my emptiness, my dirty hopelessness, rest in that thought, yes. (*Falls silent*).

MINUS: Tell me, Daddy.

DAVID: Suddenly the emptiness turns into wealth, and hopelessness into life. It's like a pardon, Minus. From sentence of death.

MINUS: Your words are terribly unreal, Daddy, but I see you mean what you say. And it makes me tremble all over. Daddy?

DAVID: Yes.

MINUS: Can it help her?

DAVID: I think so.

MINUS: Daddy.

DAVID: Yes.

MINUS: I'm shivering, my teeth are chattering, I'm shaking all over. D'you mind if I take a run?

DAVID: Take a run. I'll go and get dinner ready. See you in an hour.

Minus doesn't answer but sets off running along the shore, splashing in the water. Eventually he comes to a halt, completely out of breath. Stands and looks at the sea.

MINUS (*whispers*): Daddy spoke to me!

Winter Light
(The Communicants)

Torö
August 7, 1961. S.D.G.

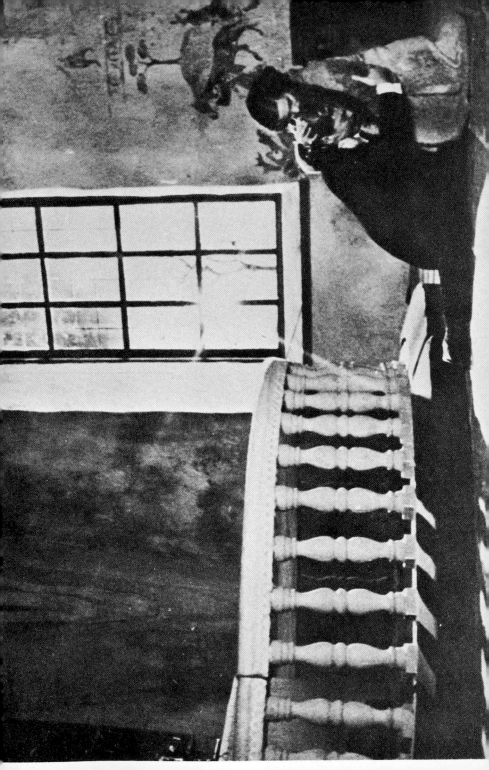

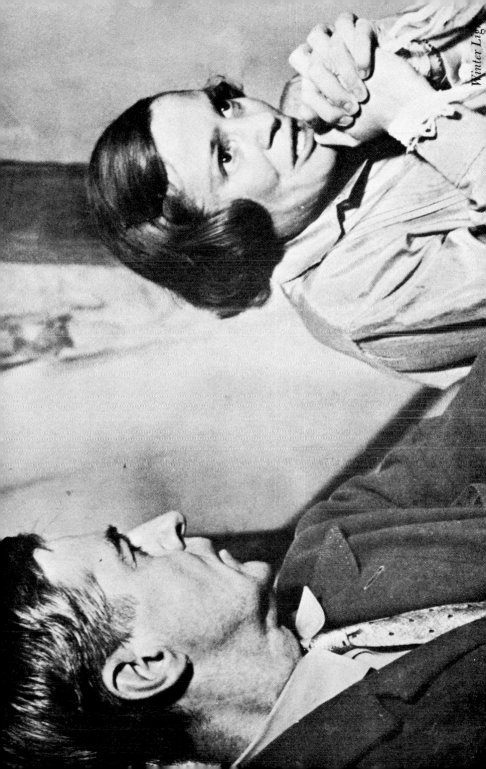

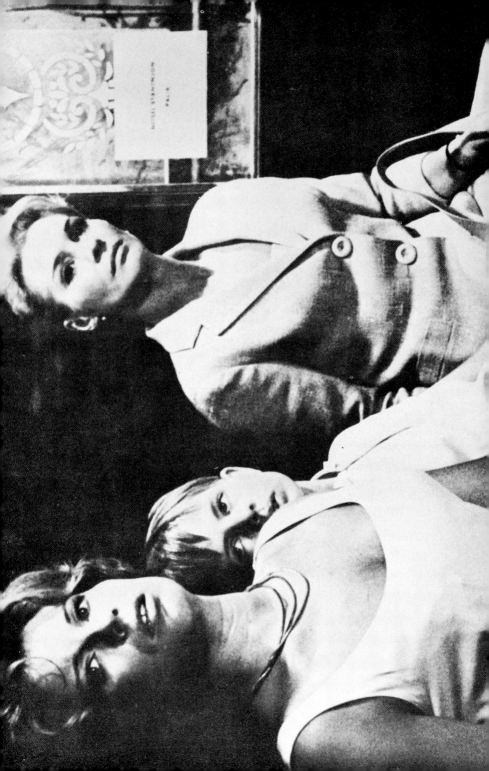

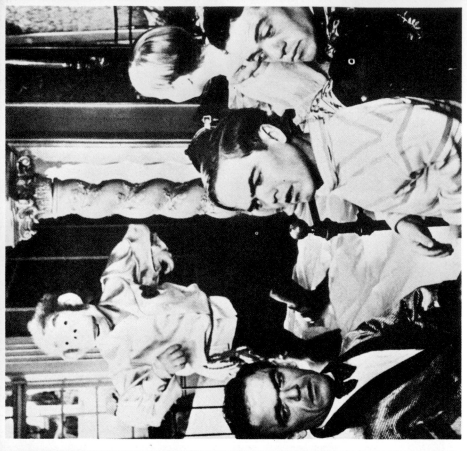

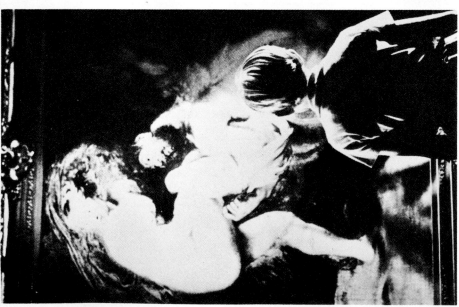

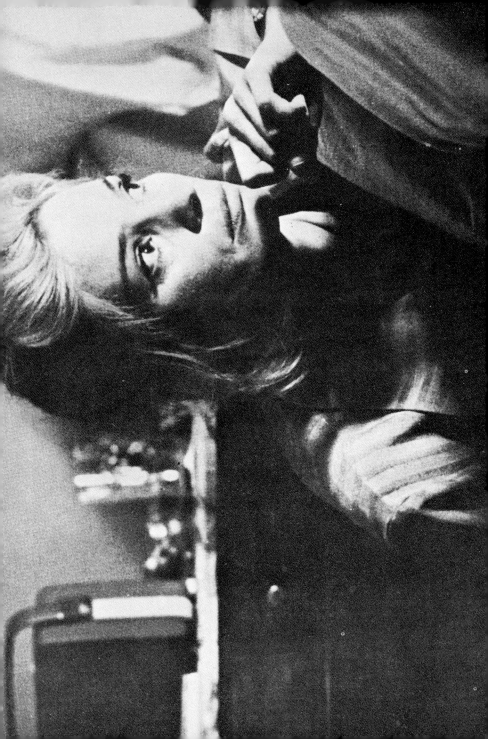

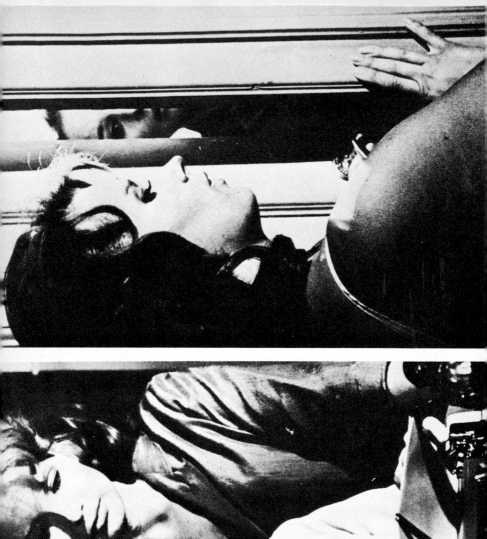

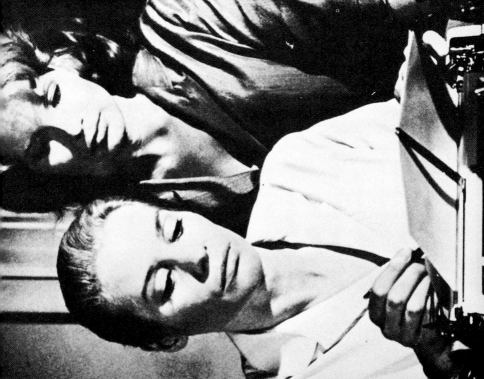

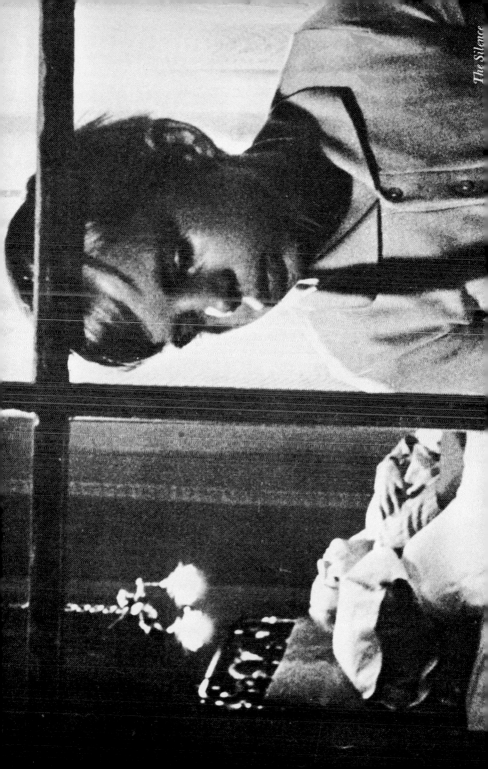

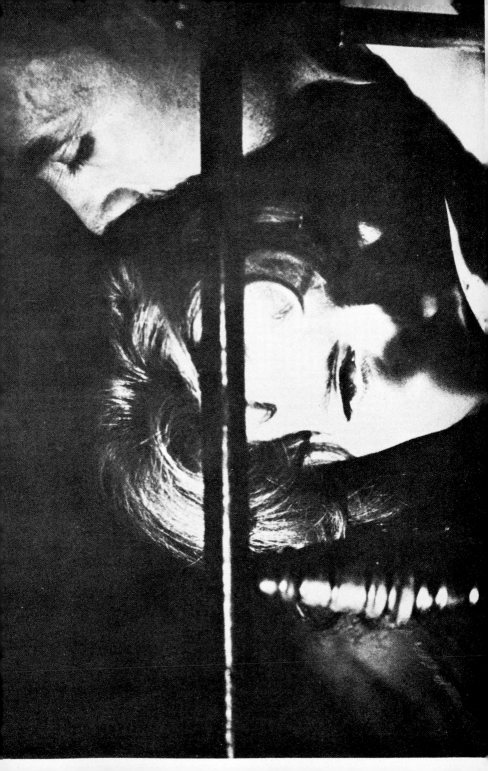

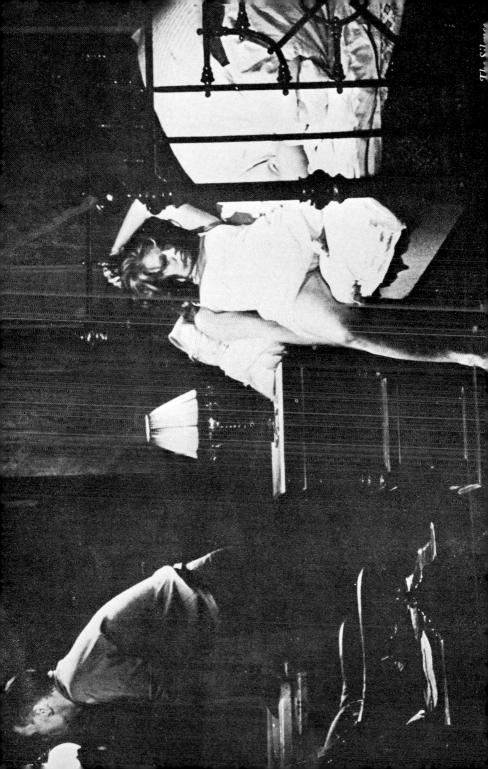

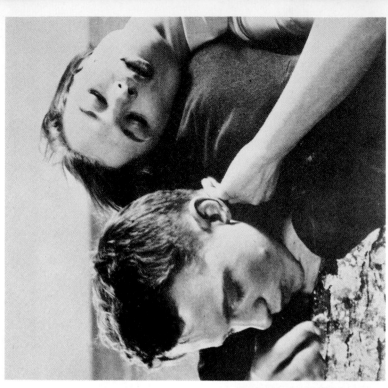

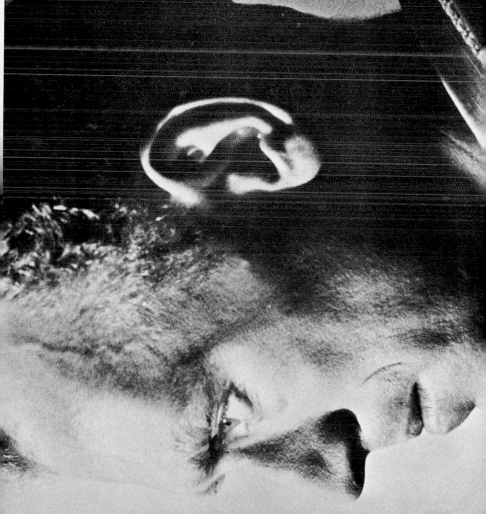

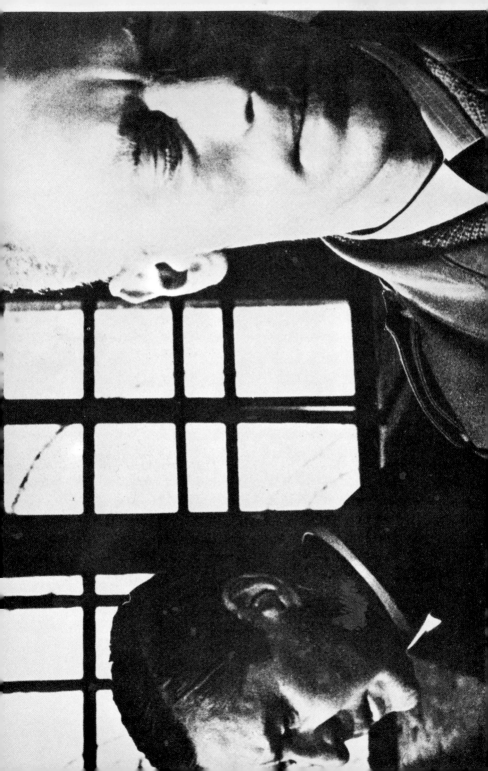

Winter Light

I

*It is twelve o'clock, midday, a Sunday at the end of November. Over the
plains, a grey half-light. A dark cold wind is blowing off the marshes to
the east.*

*Mittsunda's medieval church stands on a hill between two villages, Hol
and Djuptärn. Its parish, which comprises two hundred and sixty-seven
persons, belongs to Frostnäs rectory but has its own church council,
clergyman and elementary school.*

*A light but insistent snowfall has just begun, the earth has been frozen for
weeks and roads and fields are being swiftly covered with a greyish white
film.*

*Nine parishioners have turned up for morning service. They sit in little
groups, their expressionless faces turned toward the altar.*

*The church, though not large, is well-proportioned. The altar is a famous
piece of Flemish workmanship from the sixteenth century—a triptych with
the Holy Trinity in the centre. (Christ on the cross between the knees of
God, above them a hovering dove.) To the right cluster the apostles, to the
left the Blessed Virgin with Joseph, the Child, a cow and a donkey.*

*Against one wall, opposite the windows, a huge iron stove is hissing softly
to itself.*

It is holy communion, and the introit hymn has just been sung.

*The Rev. Tomas Eriksson turns to his congregation. He has influenza and
keeps shivering; his eyes are feverish and his forehead gleams with sweat.*

TOMAS: Lift up your hearts to God.

*The congregation gets to its feet, the organ intones the notes and the
organist sings, together with two or three of the congregation.*

THE CONGREGATION: May God lift up our hearts.

TOMAS: We give thanks unto Thee, O God.

THE CONGREGATION: He alone is worthy of thanks and praise.

*Tomas turns to the altar, reads rather quickly, in a firm voice. The
congregation remain standing.*

TOMAS: Yea, it is even right, proper and holy, in all places and
at all times, that we give thanks unto Thee and praise Thee,

65

Almighty Father, God most Holy, through Jesus Christ, our Lord.

Frail but clear, the sound of the clock in the tower is striking twelve. Tomas falls silent, raises his head, as if listening. Someone down in the church coughs, the wind presses against the big windows; outside, a black tracery of moving branches.

TOMAS (*continues*): He is the lamb of our Passover, sacrificed for us, who beareth all the world's sins, even unto death. And even as He hath overcome death and risen again and liveth for ever, so shall we and all who put their trust in Him, through Him overcome sin and death and inherit eternal life.

TOMAS (*listens*): *This silence, colorless, empty—as in a dream.* Wherefore we, with Thy faithful at all times and with all the heavenly host, praise Thy name and sing in supplication.

The organ, the little congregation and he himself try to sing these praises, this supplication.

CONGREGATION and PRIEST: Holy, holy, holy, Lord God Almighty. Heaven and earth are full of Thy glory. Give us holiness in the height. Blessed is he who cometh in the name of the Lord. Give holiness in the height.

The congregation sits down, the wooden pews bang and rumble: Johan Åkerblom, homestead owner, seventy-three years; Märta Lundberg, schoolmistress at Mittsunda elementary school, thirty-three years; Magdalena Ledfors, widow, sixty-nine (she has come three miles down the road from the village of Hol); Jonas Persson, fisherman and carpenter from Öcklarö with his wife Karin, both thirty-five; the Vicar's warden Knut Aronsson, sixty-nine; Algot Frövik, retired railway clerk, thirty-nine; Hanna Apelblad, baker, thirty-seven, with her daughter Doris, five.

TOMAS: Praise be unto Thee, Lord of heaven and earth, who hast taken pity on the children of men and given Thine only Son, that everyone who trusteth in Him shall not perish, but have eternal life.

A wave of fever passes through the clergyman's head and he draws a deep breath.

TOMAS: We thank Thee for Thy salvation, which Thou hast prepared for us through Jesus Christ. Send down Thy Holy Spirit to our hearts, that he may kindle a living faith within us and prepare us rightly to celebrate the memory of our Saviour . . .

66

He swallows, his throat is sore like an open wound.

TOMAS: . . . and receive Him, when He cometh unto us in Thy holy sacraments.

Those who know how things are done in church now bow their heads, others follow their example and Tomas reads the words instituting the communion.

TOMAS: . . . who, in the same night that He was betrayed, took bread; and when he had given thanks, he brake it, and gave it to his disciples, saying: Take, eat, this is my Body which is given for you: Do this in remembrance of me.

Algot Frövik wriggles slightly. Owing to his disability he is sitting in an uncomfortable position; he is a hunchback. The right side of his body is badly distorted, his chest flat, and his head protrudes forward. He has gentle, childlike features, but his face always wears a troubled expression, his eyes are bloodshot from insomnia.

TOMAS: Likewise after supper he took the Cup; and when he had given thanks, he gave it to them, saying, Drink ye all of this; for this is my Blood of the New Testament, which is shed for you and for many for the remission of sins; Do this, as oft as ye shall drink it, in remembrance of me. Amen.

Johan Åkerblom, who has been carefully following the text in the prayer-book, shuts it, takes off his spectacles and scratches his short-clipped grey hair with his arm.

TOMAS: Let us now pray together, even as our Lord Jesus hath taught us.

Doris Apelblad, who is only five, yawns and kicks her legs; she is like a regular pendulum. Her mother takes her hands and holds them. At the same time she grimaces disapprovingly. The pendulum stops for the moment. Tomas kneels.

TOMAS: Our Father which art in heaven, hallowed be Thy name, Thy kingdom come, Thy will be done, on earth as it is in heaven. Give us this day our daily bread and forgive us our trespasses as we forgive them that trespass against us: and lead us not into temptation, but deliver us from evil. Amen.

Tomas gets up painfully, takes the silver paten with the offerings and turns to the laity. The organ gives him a note and now, with an effort, he sings:

TOMAS (*sings*): The peace of God be with you. . . .

The congregation gets up. Most stand dumbly with expressionless faces, but Fredrik Blom, the organist, together with his wife, sings from the organ gallery.

CONGREGATION (*sings*):   O Lord God, Lamb of God, Son of the Father, that takest away the sins of the world, have mercy upon us. Thou that takest away the sins of the world, have mercy upon us. Thou that takest away the sins of the world, receive our prayer. Thou that sittest at the right hand of God the Father, have mercy upon us.

For thou only art holy; thou only art the Lord; thou only, O Christ, with the Holy Ghost, art most high in the glory of God the Father. Amen.

All sit down. There are a few moments of confusion.

Then the schoolteacher, Märta Lundberg gets up and goes forward to the altar rail. After some hesitation, Algot Frövik twists himself up onto his feet. Jonas Persson, the fisherman, fumbles with the pew door and holds it open for his wife, who is in an advanced stage of pregnancy. The old widow from Hol steps out into the aisle with firm steps and squeaking Sunday boots.

Märta Lundberg approaches the altar, stands irresolute a moment but then falls on her knees, a little to one side, on the left of the other communicants.

Tomas turns to Algot Frövik and puts the Wafer between his lips.

TOMAS: The Body of our Lord Jesus Christ, which was given for thee . . .

The old woman from Hol sticks her head out and swiftly snaps up the bread, then lets her head sink down on her breast. Tomas raises his hand in blessing.

TOMAS: The Body of our Lord Jesus Christ, which was given for thee . . .

He turns to Jonas Persson, gives him a gentle prod, the man seems absent, but jumps slightly at his touch.

TOMAS: The Body of our Lord Jesus Christ, which was given for thee . . .

Mrs. Persson takes the means of grace with quiet emotion, turns her head and looks at her husband, but he appears to be sunk in prayer.

TOMAS: The Body of our Lord Jesus Christ, which was given for thee . . . .

Finally, Tomas goes up to Märta Lundberg. Smiling ironically, she is waiting. He gives her the bread and raises his hand in blessing.

TOMAS: The Body of our Lord Jesus Christ, which was given for thee . . .

But he does not meet her glance.

Then he goes back to the altar and fetches the chalice, which he holds in his left hand, the purificator in his right. He goes down to Algot Frövik, who solemnly takes a deep gulp, swallows and nods.

TOMAS: Christ's blood, shed for thee.

The old woman lifts one hand, as if to seize the chalice; her eagerness is great; she is an habitual communicant.

TOMAS: Christ's blood, shed for thee.

He turns to Jonas Persson, who shyly lifts his head and only wets his lips with the wine.

TOMAS: Christ's blood, shed for thee.

His wife has trouble with her large ungainly body and its unaccustomed posture; moves a little clumsily and smiles apologetically at the clergyman; then obediently drinks from the chalice and clasps her hands.

TOMAS: Christ's blood, shed for thee.

Then Märta. She has laid her hands on the altar rail. He can no longer see the look in her eyes behind the thick-lensed glasses; her head is turned slightly to one side and Tomas has to wait a second or two before she deigns to notice him.

TOMAS: Christ's blood, shed for thee.

Now they have all received the bread and wine. The priest returns to the altar.

TOMAS: The grace and peace of our Lord Jesus Christ be with you all. Amen. Go, in the peace of the Lord.

The communicants get up. Jonas Persson, the fisherman, bows deeply to the Trinity above the altar. The old woman's glance strays about, she cannot quite make up her mind to go back to her pew. Mrs. Persson has difficulty in getting up. Märta gives her a hand, and they smile quickly at each other. Algot Frövik stands quite still with his eyes closed and a serious expression on his face, from which the pain has departed. He seems quietly satisfied.

Then they go back to their places. Tomas cautiously clears his throat; it is very sore.

TOMAS: Let us pray.

He turns to the altar, reads from the book.

TOMAS: We thank Thee, Almighty Father, who through Thy Son, Jesus Christ, hast instituted this holy communion, to our consolation and bliss. We pray Thee: Give us grace so to

69

commemorate Jesus on earth, that we may be partakers in
Thy great communion in heaven.

*Blom, the precentor and organist, with his wife and Algot Frövik, sings
a powerful "Amen". Tomas turns to the congregation.*

TOMAS: Give thanks and praise unto the Lord.

*The congregation get up and the organ puffs and squeaks. Someone drops
a walking stick on the floor.*

THE CONGREGATION (*sings*): Praise and thanks be unto the
Lord. Halleluja, halleluja, halleluja.

*Some sit down, but the vicar's warden and Algot Frövik remain standing—
which causes those who have sat down to get up again.*

The wooden pews bang and thud.

TOMAS: Bow down your hearts to God and receive His blessing.
The Lord bless you and preserve you, the Lord let the light
of His countenance shine upon you and be gracious unto
you. The Lord turn His face toward you and give you
peace. In the name of God the Father, God the Son and
God the Holy Ghost. Amen.

THE CONGREGATION (*singing*): Amen, Amen, Amen.

*The organ abruptly modulates into the last hymn, which is number four
hundred, verse eleven:*

Last, my God, I pray Thee,/Take my hand in Thine/
Lead me, gently lead me,/To the land divine,/
And when woes are ended,/And my course is run/
Thou wilt take my spirit/Home, O Lord, to Thine.

*A few moments of stillness follow this chorale. Doris's mother snaps shut
the clasp of her handbag and wakes her sleeping daughter. The service is
over. Precipitately, Fredrik Blom performs his voluntary.*

*Tomas goes out to the vestry, followed by the warden Aronsson, who is
carrying the collection in a bag on the end of a pole. He empties its scanty
contents onto the table and counts the coins (four kronor and thirty-six öre)
collects the money into another little bag, which he pedantically ties up.
Then writes down the amount in the cashbook provided for the
purpose.*

*Meanwhile Tomas has freed himself from his chasuble and sat down in
a little leather armchair. He looks inside his brief-case and brings out a
Thermos flask and a packet of biscuits, pouring out his coffee into a large
cracked cup.*

ARONSSON: You look poorly.

TOMAS: If I could only go home to bed.

70

ARONSSON: Can't you ring up Broms and ask him to take the three-o'clock service at Frostnäs?

TOMAS: He's out for a spin in his new car.

ARONSSON: You've caught a dose of 'flu.

TOMAS: It's my throat that's worst.

He sips his coffee cautiously. Aronsson has put on his glasses, leans over whatever it is he is writing.

ARONSSON: Tomas!

TOMAS: Yes?

ARONSSON: How did it turn out?

TOMAS: What?

ARONSSON: Did you get a housekeeper?

TOMAS: No.

ARONSSON: You won't be able to manage on your own in the long run, you know.

TOMAS: Can and can't. I've done it for five years, I can do it a while longer.

Tomas chews a biscuit, chews and swallows. Aronsson brings out a big handkerchief, polishes his spectacles.

ARONSSON: You could ask Märta Lundberg to help you. She'd like nothing better. I'll ask her.

TOMAS: No thanks.

And that's that. Aronsson has failed. He gets up and hangs up the chasuble in the cupboard. Tomas has stretched his legs out and sunk down in his chair. He closes his eyes, his parched lips are slightly cracked.

Algot Frövik steps into the vestry; out of mere politeness he gives a tap at the door but, with the air of being one of the elect, of belonging to those who dwell behind the veil, enters.

ALGOT: Good morning, Vicar, hallo, Aronsson. How are you? Thanks for the sermon.

TOMAS: Good morning, Mr. Frövik. Thank you.

ARONSSON: Hallo, Frövik.

Algot is slightly at a loss. He becomes shy, can't think what to say, smiles apologetically.

TOMAS: Something special you wanted, Mr. Frövik?

ALGOT: No, no. I thought maybe I could be of some use. (*Pause*) And then there was one thing. . . Could I have a word with you, Vicar?

TOMAS: We'll be seeing each other at Frostnäs at three o'clock, won't we?

71

ALGOT: And you'll have time to speak to me then?

TOMAS: Of course. After service.

ALGOT: I'll be in church an hour before, to turn the heating up. Same hymns?

TOMAS (*nods*).

ALGOT: You're not quite well, Vicar?

TOMAS (*impatiently*): No, I've some sort of a cold.

ALGOT: Well, it's this weather. For my part . . .

Realizing no one is just now interested in his personal aches and pains, he silently takes his leave. Bowing, he withdraws.

TOMAS: Poor wretch.

ARONSSON: He has his pension from the railway. As well as something from the Church Council for helping out at Frostnäs, I suppose?

Aronsson gives his habitual dignified sigh. Tomas yawns, feels his throat. It's sore. Feverish, he closes his eyes.

ARONSSON: You've got a visitor.

Tomas opens his eyes again. In the doorway a glimpse of Jonas Persson and his wife.

ARONSSON: Mrs. Persson feels she must at all costs have a word with you.

Mrs. Persson, not waiting for an answer, steps in.

MRS. PERSSON: I've got to speak to you, Vicar.

TOMAS: Of course. Yes.

He turns to the man, makes a sign. Hesitantly he follows her, stops inside the door and bows, first to Aronsson, then to the Vicar. (Jonas Persson is a tall, thin fellow with a face that might be carved out of wood. Two terrified eyes stare painfully out of this face. His thin wispy hair has started to go grey, but his mouth is weak and childish. Mrs. Persson has thick dark hair. Her face has breadth and obstinacy, but her glance, too, is anxious.)

Tomas gets up and offers them his hand, asks them to sit down. Aronsson takes his hat, winds his woollen scarf round his neck, slips on his galoshes and takes his leave.

ARONSSON: I'll ring this evening, in case you want anything.

TOMAS: Thanks, but there's really no need.

ARONSSON: Good-bye, Mr. Persson, good-bye, Mrs. Persson.

THE PERSSONS: Good-bye.

Aronsson goes off through the outside door of the vestry. A grey cold draft sweeps through the room.

The clergyman looks at his two visitors. Jonas Persson has placed his elbow on the table and rubs the tip of one finger incessantly against his cheek; his glance is averted, as if to spare his fellow beings its look of terror. Mrs. Persson leans forward, presses her stomach hard against the edge of the table. But finds no words.

TOMAS: You wished to speak to me.

MRS. PERSSON: Yes. Though it wasn't quite like that either. It was Jonas, really, though he says nothing. So I thought . . . this morning I thought we'd come to church. And speak to someone else.

JONAS: We're at our wits' end.

MRS. PERSSON: At our wits' end. (*Nods*) That's to say Jonas is. Not me so much. But Jonas is . . .

She turns to her husband. He does not let her see how frightened he is, looks down at the table.

MRS. PERSSON: Can't you speak to Jonas, Vicar?

TOMAS: Yes, of course.

Tomas looks at the man's face.

TOMAS (*cautiously*): Has this troubled you long, Mr. Persson?

Jonas Persson rubs his finger against his cheek.

MRS. PERSSON: It all began last spring. Jonas had read in the papers about the Chinese.

Uncertainly she looks at her husband. But he just sits as before, though he has moved away slightly from the clergyman and from his wife. Tomas inclines his head, feigning an attempt to sympathize and understand.

MRS. PERSSON: It said in the paper that the Chinese are being brought up to hate.

Tomas nods again, encouragingly.

MRS. PERSSON: They've nothing to eat, or anyway very little. They become soldiers and train for war.

Jonas Persson stops rubbing his cheek with his finger. He lays his hands on the table.

MRS. PERSSON: In the article it said that . . . It's just a *question of time* until the Chinese have atom bombs. *They've nothing to lose.* That's what it said. (*Pause*) I don't worry too much. That must be because I haven't much imagination. But Jonas thinks about it all the time. We turn the matter over this way and that. Though, of course, I can't be of much help. We've three children—besides the one who's on the way, of course.

She falls silent, looking to the Vicar, her help and support, for an answer. She is entrusting him with her husband's life, waiting for the word which will dissolve this Chinese threat and disentangle her existence.

TOMAS: We all go with the same dread—more or less.

Helplessly, Tomas looks at Jonas Persson's hard brow and knotted eyebrows.

TOMAS: We must trust in God.

Jonas Persson slowly raises his head and looks at Tomas. Anxiety flashes through him like an electric shock, a physical blow.

He grabs the cup and noisily gulps down what is left of the coffee, now cold.

The fisherman no longer turns away his glance, is no longer considerate, spares no one. His wife puts her hands up and takes off her hat, smoothing out her thick hair with the flats of her hands.

TOMAS: We live our simple daily lives. And then some terrible piece of information forces itself into our secure, safe world. It's more than we can bear. The whole state of affairs is so overwhelming, God becomes so remote.

Jonas, smiling, shakes his head. He seems to pity them.

MRS. PERSSON (*dubiously*): Yes, yes.

TOMAS: I feel so helpless. I don't know what to say. I understand your fear, God, how I understand it! But we must go on living.

JONAS: Why must we go on living?

TOMAS: Because we must. We have a responsibility.

JONAS: You aren't well, Vicar, and I shouldn't sit here talking. Anyway we won't get anywhere.

TOMAS (*anxiously*): Yes! Let's talk to each other. Let's say whatever comes into our heads.

The fisherman looks at the vicar in astonishment, then slowly shakes his head. The pitying smile returns.

JONAS: It's impossible.

TOMAS: Impossible?

JONAS: Karin and I've got to get back to the children. They're all alone. One never knows what they might be up to.

MRS. PERSSON: Drive me home, then, and come back to the vicar. It's much better if you're alone together.

TOMAS: When can you get back?

MRS. PERSSON: It'll only take us ten minutes to get home.

TOMAS: In half an hour you'll be back here. *Promise me that.*

74

Silently, Jonas gets up. His wife takes his hand, as if wishing to extort a promise from him.

MRS.PERSSON: Promise the vicar you'll come back.

JONAS (*embarrassed*): Of course . . . I promise.

They take their farewell, quickly and awkwardly. Tomas unlocks the outer door, holds it open.

TOMAS: Is your car parked outside?

MRS.PERSSON: It's just down at the corner.

TOMAS: I'll be waiting. And Mr. Persson will be back in half an hour, at the outside.

MRS.PERSSON: I'll see he returns.

TOMAS: The main door is open. You can come in through the church. I'll be waiting for you here.

Jonas Persson nods and braces himself against the wind in the open doorway. His wife follows him out. Tomas shuts the door and locks it.

After a few moments he sees them get into their car. It reverses and turns cautiously down toward the main road.

The gale has grown stronger, and it is half-past twelve.

Tomas goes out into the church, stands absent-mindedly in front of the altar: Christ on the cross, between God's knees. God himself has black hair and a brown beard and eyebrows arched as if in surprise. The dove flutters above His head.

TOMAS (*to himself*): What a ridiculous image!

Feeling himself observed, he turns round.

TOMAS: Oh, I see, it's you.

Märta is standing at the far end, by the entrance. In her hand she holds a basket.

MÄRTA: Here, I've something hot for you.

TOMAS: Thanks. Kind of you. Actually I've brought some coffee from home.

He walks away from her. She follows him into the vestry.

TOMAS: I'm waiting for someone who wants to speak to me. He may be here any moment.

MÄRTA: Don't worry. I'll be gone in a moment.

She puts the basket on a chair, unbuttons her sheepskin coat, fumbles in her pocket, takes out a handkerchief and blows her nose.

MÄRTA: It's really turning cold.

Tomas goes up to the little prison window of the vestry, leans his elbows on its broad stone sill. She stands beside him, puts her arm round his shoulder and draws him to herself.

75

MÄRTA: Poor Tomas.

Her compassionate, gentle tone of voice, his fever, a feeling of foreboding. His eyelids swell, redden.

MÄRTA: What is it, Tomas?

TOMAS: To you, nothing.

MÄRTA: Tell me, even so.

TOMAS: God's silence.

MÄRTA (*wonderingly*): God's silence?

TOMAS: Yes. (*Long pause*) God's silence.

She leans her head against his shoulder, her beret slips askew, drops to the floor. They look at the snow, falling ever more thickly.

Both the thicket on the other side of the road and the yard are gradually disappearing.

TOMAS: Then along come Jonas Persson and his wife.

He presses one fist against his mouth and his body is shaken by coughing.

TOMAS: I talked a lot of drivel. Cut off from God. Yet I had a feeling every word I said was—decisive. What am I to do!

MÄRTA: Poor Tomas! What you need is a brandy and to be put to bed. You've got a high temperature.

Märta lays her large hand against his temple, he lets her be—her hand is cool, anyway.

TOMAS: Why did you come to Communion?

MÄRTA: It's supposed to be a love-feast, isn't it? (*Pause*) By the way, have you read my letter?

TOMAS: Letter? No. I haven't had time.

Märta takes away her hand and smiles ironically.

MÄRTA: You're hopeless. When did you get it?

TOMAS (*truthfully*): Yesterday. I sat and wrote my sermon, and it was a very thick letter, wasn't it? Anyway I thought . . .

MÄRTA: What did you think?

TOMAS: That it was something unpleasant. I've got it with me.

He feels for his pocket, she shakes her head.

MÄRTA: No, no. Read it later. Sometime when you feel like it.

TOMAS: Why do you write, when we see each other every day?

MÄRTA: We go astray when we talk. Don't look so terrified.

Tomas lets go the thread of the conversation, hasn't the strength to explain, every syllable makes his throat ache. He yawns like a sleepy child and lays his head in his arms.

MÄRTA (*smiling*): A Sunday at the very bottom of the vale of tears.

76

TOMAS: I don't feel too well.

MÄRTA: Want me to be sorry for you?

TOMAS: Yes, please.

MÄRTA (*smiles*): Then you'll have to marry me.

TOMAS (*sighs, closes his eyes*): Oh, I see.

MÄRTA: You could so easily marry me.

TOMAS: What for?

MÄRTA: Then I wouldn't have to go away from here. For example.

TOMAS: Why have you got to go away from here?

MÄRTA: As long as I'm only a temporary they can move me where they like. Far away. (*Smiling*) From you.

TOMAS (*very tired*): We'll see what we'll do . . .

MÄRTA (*hastily, still smiling*): Yes, yes, I know. You can't marry me because you don't love me. Besides which I don't believe in God. No, I don't believe in God a bit. And that's the truth.

Tomas looks out of the window.

Blom, the organist, is struggling up the hill toward the church, red in the face from the wind. Presumably he has forgotten something in the vestry.

MÄRTA: Why don't you say something?

TOMAS: Because you never stop talking. Anyway I've heard it all before. At least once a year.

Märta gives a slightly bitter laugh and thumps him in the back with her hand.

MÄRTA: You don't know what's good for you. Marry me, and you'll have a good wife. A faithful one, too. After all, I'm not exactly beautiful, so you can have me to yourself.

A sound of hasty footsteps, someone clears his throat, Tomas and Märta move apart from one another. Blom, the organist, steps into the vestry, he is covered in snow and irritable, looks at them, laughs.

BLOM: Beg your pardon, but I must be off, to play at a christening, and I've forgotten my music. Sorry I disturbed you, sorry. Good morning, Miss Lundberg. As a matter of fact, I was going to speak to you about the boy, but just now I'm in a hurry. It's not every day one has a chance of earning a bit extra in this hole. 'Undskyld'* as the Danes say. Where the deuce have I put that music! There it is. Look, there's the whole heap. Bye, then, Miss Lundberg. Bye, Tomas.

* You must excuse me.

77

His laugh is faintly libellous. These ageing people with their anxious faces and surreptitious feelings! (He, Blom, at least has been right through himself and the whole sorry business. Even so, he goes on living and labors in his calling: music to the glory of God. Besides, he's a personality, and gladly admits he is always in better form in the afternoon than in the morning.)

MÄRTA: I must go. Aunt Emma's come to see me. She's going to bake a cake (*sighs*) for tea.

TOMAS: Märta.

MÄRTA: Yes, Tomas.

She puts on her fur, retrieves her beret which has fallen to the floor. Then she picks up her basket with the coffee, off the chair, and puts it on the table.

TOMAS: Supposing he doesn't come. I mean Jonas Persson?

MÄRTA: Then you can go home, can't you, and rest up a bit. (*Mocking*) And read my letter.

TOMAS: No, you don't understand.

MÄRTA: There's your coffee.

She goes toward the door, on the way she lays a hand on Tomas's arm.

TOMAS: What do you want now?

MÄRTA: Poor Tomas. Really, I mean it. And here I come and am nasty to you.

TOMAS (*impatient*): Oh, you're welcome.

MÄRTA (*irritated*): Sometimes I think you're the limit! God's silence, God doesn't speak. God hasn't ever spoken, because he doesn't exist. It's all so unusually, horribly simple.

She bends down and kisses him on the mouth and the cheek. She is desperately sad.

TOMAS: Now you'll get the 'flu.

MÄRTA (*ironically*): And like having it, of course, having caught it from you.—Shall I stay?

TOMAS: No thanks. No need.

MÄRTA: Oh, Tomas, what a lot you've still to learn.

TOMAS (*sarcastically*): Is that what you teach your pupils?

MÄRTA (*same tone of voice*): You must learn to love.

TOMAS (*same tone of voice*): And I suppose it's you who're going to teach me?

Märta looks at him a long while, then shakes her head and gives a wry smile.

MÄRTA: It's beyond me. I haven't the strength.

She leaves him, goes out through the church. He hears the doors slam behind her.

II

Opposite the vestry window hangs a crucifix. It is a crude, roughly carved image of the suffering Christ, ineptly made. The mouth opens in a scream, the arms are grotesquely twisted, the hands convulsively clutch the nails, the brow is bloody beneath the thorns, and the body arches outwards, as if trying to tear itself away from the wood. The image smells of fungus, moldy timber. Its paint is flaking off in long strips.
Over in the corner the clock ticks, on the wall. It has its own secret life. Against the shorter wall stands a big cupboard, lavishly decorated with carved figures in all the rich and swelling exuberance of the baroque. Its door is half open; inside, a glimpse of waxen yellow silk of chasubles used for the church festivals.

TOMAS: He must come. After all he came to Communion.

The clock pauses, sighs; and then hard, resounding it strikes: one.

TOMAS: He must come!

Imagining he hears footsteps in the church, he hurries out to meet Jonas; but it's only an aural illusion. The church is empty in the twilight of the winter afternoon.
Inside the iron stove the fire whines and mutters, while between the two halves of the main door the gale whistles, full of distress.
On the wall opposite the stove hangs some noble family's ponderous coat of arms, with helm, visor, sword, bones and a death's head.
The snow, falling in a grey sleet, runs down the window panes.
He goes back to the vestry, opens his wallet and takes out Märta's letter, lays it open in front of him on the table. In one of the pockets is a photo of his wife.
Illness has already marked her down and emaciated her, her eyes are frightened and restless: Mrs. Anna Magdalena Ericsson, twenty-seven, four months and twelve days. May the Lord teach us so to think upon our own impending demise that, when at the last we come to be parted from this transient life, we may be prepared to leave it in the odour of sanctity.
The funeral bell. The great bell creaks, then strikes. His wife is dead, but Tomas is in the hands of God, all doubt is silenced and his uncertainty dissolves itself in a triumphant cry: "God has stricken me!"
His wife's photo. In the margin: "To my husband on his forty-seventh birthday". *Her mouth is bitter and twisted and her throat has two jagged scars after her operations.*

TOMAS: Dearest.

He lays his hand over the picture, puts it back in his wallet, sees Märta's letter, bulky and commanding.

He takes a grip on himself, rips open the envelope and unfolds the sheets of untidily folded notepaper:

We find it so hard to talk to each other. We are both rather shy people, and I become all too easily sarcastic. That's why I'm writing to you, as I have something to tell you which seems important.

Do you remember last summer? I had eczema on both hands and everything was so wretched. One evening we were in the church together, arranging flowers on the altar. There was to be a confirmation. Do you remember what a particularly difficult time I was going through, just then, with both hands bandaged and unable to sleep at night from the irritation—my skin had flaked off and my palms were like open sores. There we stood, busy with marguerites and cornflowers (or whatever they were) and I felt terribly irritable. Suddenly, feeling angry with you, I asked you, out of sheer malice, about the efficacy of prayer, and whether you believed in it. Naturally, you replied you did. Maliciously, again, I asked whether you had prayed for my hands and you said no, it was a thing you hadn't thought of. I became very melodramatic. Suggested you should pray for me there and then. Oddly enough, you agreed. This compliance made me even more angry, I tore off the bandage—well, you remember. The open sores affected you unpleasantly. You couldn't pray, the whole situation simply disgusted you. Now, after the event, I understand you; but you never understood me. After all, we'd been living together quite a while, almost two years. One would think this represented a certain little capital in our poverty, in tendernesses exchanged, and in our clumsy attempts to get round the lovelessness of our relationship. And then, when the eczema broke out on my forehead and around my scalp, it wasn't long before I noticed you were avoiding me. You found me distasteful, even though you were considerate about it and didn't want to hurt my feelings. Then the disease flamed up on my hands and feet. And our relationship ended. For me it was a frightful shock and an extra painful strain on my nerves. Hence all my nasty remarks, my irony, my sarcasms. After all, I'd been given incontrovertible proof we didn't love each other—a fact we could no longer run away from, or close our eyes to.

I have never believed in your faith. Chiefly, of course, because I've never been tormented by religious temptation. I grew up in a non-Christian family, full of warmth and kindness and loyalty—and joy. God and Christ didn't exist, except as vague notions. And when I came into contact with your faith, it seemed to me obscure and neurotic, in some way cruelly overcharged with emotion, primitive. One thing in particular I couldn't understand, your peculiar indifference to the gospels and to Jesus Christ.

And now, anyway, I must tell you of a strange case of prayer being heard. If you're in the mood it'll give you a good laugh. Personally, of course, I don't believe there was the remotest connection, life is problematic enough as it is, I mean without supernatural factors. Our so-called commonsense has quite enough on its plate with the psychological and biological nonsense.

Well, you recall how you were going to pray for my eczema but—though afterwards you denied it—were struck dumb by distaste. Half out of my wits, I wanted still further to exasperate you—I saw your terrified face close to me. Remember how I said: Quiet! Since you can't pray for me, I'll pray for myself.

God, I said to myself, why have you created me so eternally dissatisfied, so frightened, so bitter? Why must I understand how wretched I am, why have I got to suffer as in the hell of my own indifference? If there is a purpose in my suffering, then tell me what it is! And I'll bear my pain without complaining. I'm strong. You've made me so terribly strong, both in body and soul, but you give me nothing to do with my strength. Give me a meaning to my life, and I'll be your obedient slave! More or less, that's what I prayed. Afterwards I didn't give the matter another thought—became slightly hysterical and made things unpleasant for you, my poor Tomas.

Well, it was all about as melodramatic as could be, but that eczema was really very irritating.

This autumn, I've realized my prayer has been heard. And here's your cue to laugh. I prayed for clarity of mind, and I got it. I've realized I love you. I prayed for a task to apply my strength to, and got it, too. It's you.

Such thoughts can pass through the head of a schoolteacher of an evening when the telephone doesn't ring and it's dark and lonely.

Whether it's God or my biological functions which have brought about my love for you, anyway I'm burning with gratitude. Nor does it make any odds whether it's my inborn tendency to assume responsibility for others that tempts me to find in you my great task in life, since it can't do you any harm—you can't be more damaged than you are already.

What I lack entirely is the capacity to show you my love. I haven't the remotest idea how to go about it. I've been so miserable I've even thought of praying another prayer. But I still have a little self-respect left, in spite of all, some feelings of decency.

Dearest Tomas—this has turned out to be a long letter. But now I've written what I don't dare to say even when you're in my arms: I love you and I live for you. Take me and use me. Beneath all my false pride and independent airs I've only one wish: to be allowed to live for someone else. It will be terribly difficult.

When I think the matter over, I can't understand how it is to happen. Maybe it's all a mistake. Dearest, tell me it's not a mistake.

Tomas reads the letter to the end, here and there takes a few lines over again, folds up its many pages of large obstinately sloping hand-writing, and stuffs them back into the envelope which gets torn at one corner.

He puts the letter into his brief-case, takes it out again, holds it in his hand, puts it into his wallet; but there's no more room for it there. Irritated, he pokes it down into his overcoat pocket.

He sits down at the table, drumming with his fingers; feels overwhelmingly sleepy, blinks, passes a hand over his face.

Suddenly Jonas Persson is there. He is standing just inside the door, holding his snow-soaked hat in his hand. His face is very damp and pale. He breathes deeply, as if he'd been running.

TOMAS: I'm glad you've come. So glad you . . . It's been a long wait.

JONAS: I'm sorry I'm late.

TOMAS: No, not that. I didn't mean it as a reproach. Won't you take your coat off? I've some hot coffee here. And two cups.

Without taking off his coat Jonas Persson sits down at the table. He is still holding his hat in his hand. He declines the coffee, but when Tomas insists and pours it out, sips it politely.

TOMAS: Can't be out on the water very long at this time of year, eh?

JONAS: No, just short trips, and that's a fact.

TOMAS: Got much to do ashore?

JONAS: I'm building a new boat, over at Törnström's yard.

TOMAS: Yes, of course. An excellent yard, I had my own boat built there. At Törnström's yard, that is.

End of conversation. Jonas stares at the table and again Tomas feels his ineffectuality sweeping over him, leaving him paralysed and in a cold sweat.

TOMAS: Have you got money worries?

JONAS *(shakes his head, smiles)*.

TOMAS: Well, forgive me for asking. But such things can drive a man to despair.

JONAS *(politely)*: Yes, of course. Obviously. As we know.

Tomas clasps his hands so that the knuckles gleam. A pain throbs behind his eyes and his mouth is dry. The giddy feeling comes and goes, through head and stomach.

TOMAS: How long have you—er—been going about with this idea of taking your own life?

JONAS: Don't know. A long time, I think.

TOMAS: Have you spoken to a doctor?

JONAS *(astonished)*.

TOMAS: Often one can . . . I mean . . . Well. D'you get on all right with your wife? I've the impression . . .

JONAS: Karin's all right. She's all right.

TOMAS: And so it all comes down to this business with the Chinese, who . . .

JONAS *(tormented)*: Yes.

TOMAS: But after all if it happens, Mr. Persson, it'll hit us all. We're all responsible; and we must all take the consequences.

JONAS *(frightened)*.

TOMAS: There are still tremendous possibilities that war will be avoided. Those of us who can see the danger mustn't just sit and wait for the catastrophe to happen. We must fight it, tooth and nail, do everything we can to support the forces of peace.

JONAS (*looks out of the window*).

They fall silent, and the old clock on the wall limps, hesitates, clears its throat. It is eight minutes past one.

TOMAS: Jonas, listen to me a moment. I'll speak openly to you, without reservations. You know my wife died four years ago. I loved her. My life was at an end, I'm not frightened of death, there isn't the least reason for me to go on living.

JONAS (*a glimmer of interest*).

TOMAS: I was left behind. Not for my own sake, but to be of some use.

JONAS (*nods slowly*).

TOMAS: Believe me, I had great dreams once. I was going to make my mark in the world. Well, you know the sort of ideas you get when you're young. My mother protected me from everything evil, everything ugly, everything dangerous. Of cruelty or evil I knew absolutely nothing. When I was ordained I was as innocent as a babe in arms. Then everything happened at once. For a while I was seaman's pastor in Lisbon. It was during the Spanish Civil War. We had a front seat in the stalls. But I refused to see, or understand. I refused to accept reality. I and my God lived in one world, a specially arranged world, where everything made sense. All round were the agonies of real life. But I didn't see them. I turned my gaze toward my God.

JONAS (*distressed, restive*).

TOMAS: Forgive me for talking about myself. Please don't misunderstand me. All I mean is, we, you and I, in our different ways, have shut ourselves in and locked the door behind us. You with your fear and I——

JONAS (*questioning, tormented*).

TOMAS: Please, you *must* understand. I'm no good as a clergyman. I chose my calling because my mother and father were religious, pious, in a deep and natural way. Maybe I didn't really love them, but I wanted to please them. So I became a clergyman and believed in God. (*Gives a short laugh*) An improbable, entirely private, fatherly god. Who loved mankind, of course, but most of all me.

Tomas is overcome by a violent attack of coughing and has to get up. He draws a deep breath, grimaces.

TOMAS: A god who guaranteed me every imaginable security. Against fear of death. Against fear of life. A god I'd suggested myself into believing in, a god I'd borrowed from various quarters, fabricated with my own hands. D'you understand, Jonas? What a monstrous mistake I'd made? Can you realize what a bad priest must come of such a spoiled, shut-in, anxious wretch as me?

JONAS *(more and more anxious)*.

TOMAS *(eagerly)*: Can you imagine my prayers? To an echo-god. Who gave benign answers and reassuring blessings?

JONAS *(tense)*.

TOMAS: Every time I confronted God with the reality I saw, he became ugly, revolting, a spider god—a monster. That's why I hid him away from the light, from life. In my darkness and loneliness I hugged him to myself—the only person I showed him to was my wife. She backed me up, encouraged me, helped me, plugged up all the holes. Our dreams. *(He gives a sudden laugh)*.

JONAS *(more and more terrified)*.

TOMAS: My indifference to the gospel message, my jealous hatred of Jesus.

JONAS *(looks away)*: I'd better be going along now.

TOMAS: No. *(Frightened)* No. *(Frightened)* No, you mustn't go! You've got to understand why I'm telling you all this about myself. I want you to see what a poor sort of human being, what a bankrupt wretch it is, who's sitting here before you. I'm not a priest. I'm a beggar who needs your help!

JONAS *(anxiously)*: I'm very grateful to you, sir, for giving me so much of your valuable time, and for saying such nice things to me. But now I must be going along. Otherwise Karin will be wondering where I've got to and . . . and will be getting worried.

TOMAS: Just a little longer. Five minutes . . . Just . . .

JONAS *(sits down, extremely restive)*.

TOMAS: That's right. Now let's have a nice quiet talk. Forgive me—I've been talking in a confused, incomprehensible way.

But such a lot of things can suddenly come over one, can't they?

Tomas gets up from the table and shuts the church door, standing beneath the crucifix.

JONAS (*trapped*).

TOMAS: Well, and what if God doesn't exist? What difference does it make?

JONAS (*looks towards the door*).

TOMAS: Life becomes something we can understand. What a relief! And death—extinction, dissolution of body and soul. People's cruelty, their loneliness, their fear—everything becomes self-evident—transparent. Suffering is incomprehensible, so it needn't be explained. The stars out in space, worlds, heavens, all have given birth to themselves and to each other. There isn't any creator, no one who holds it all together, no immeasurable thought to make one's head spin.

JONAS (*looks towards the door*).

TOMAS: We're alone, you and I. We've betrayed the only condition under which men can live: to live together. And that's why we're so poverty-stricken, joyless and full of fear. All this stink of an antique godliness! All this supernatural helplessness, this humiliating sense of sin!

JONAS (*averts his glance*).

TOMAS: You must live, Jonas. Summer's on the way. After all, the darkness won't last for ever. You've got your strawberry beds, haven't you, and your flowering jasmine? What perfume! Long hot days. It's the earthly paradise, Jonas. It's something to live for!

JONAS (*looks at the wall*).

TOMAS: We'll see a lot of each other, you and I. We'll become good friends, and talk to each other about this dark day. We've given gifts to each other, haven't we? You've given me your fear and I've given you a god I've killed.

JONAS (*looks away*).

TOMAS: I don't feel well, I've got a fever. Everything's swaying about. I . . . I can't collect my thoughts. I'm ill. The fact is, I'm in a wretched state.

He lays his arms on the table and supports his forehead on his hands. Shaken by feverish chills, he moans faintly, the sweat breaks out on his

forehead and temples and on his hands. Gradually the attack subsides. He
becomes quieter. When he looks up Jonas has vanished. No footsteps, no
sound of a door closing. No wind in cracks and crevices. Complete
silence. He drags himself over to the window.
No car, no traces. Not a sound. The snow falls softly and steadily.
God's silence, Christ's twisted face, the blood on the brow and hands, the
soundless shriek behind the bared teeth.
God's silence.

TOMAS (*moaning*):   God, my God, why have you abandoned me?
He steps out into the chancel. It's half-past one and the sun breaks through
the snow-cloud. Resting on the low hills beyond the forest, it casts a heavy
red light into the silence, striking on stone walls, old coats of arms of the
nobility hung up there, the pulpit's gilded woodwork and the vestry's
dark abyss.
A dull silence fills the great spaces of the church. Beneath the crossed vanes
of the vaulting, it presses against the gallery's carved prophets, weighs
down upon the stone paving slabs and the half-illegible inscriptions of
tombs in the floor. After life has fled. The last moment.
Tomas falls on his knees, then on his face, at full length on the stone
floor. Then raises himself on the palms of his hands, half gets up, gasping
for breath.

TOMAS: No. (*Pause*) God does not exist any more.
He gets to his feet, stands motionless, listening. The sudden sunshine
dazzles him. He is giddy, breathless.

TOMAS: I'm free now. At last, free.
That moment he catches sight of Märta. She is standing just behind the
pulpit, out of the sunshine. Exhausted, he sits down in one of the pews in
the chancel. A long pause.

TOMAS: Did anyone see you going out of here?
MÄRTA: No.
TOMAS: Have you just come in, or have you been here long?
MÄRTA: When I left you, I thought I'd go home. But regretted
       it. So I came back into the vestry and I saw you were
       asleep at the table. I didn't want to disturb you. So I de-
       cided to wait out here.
TOMAS: You haven't seen Jonas Persson?
MÄRTA (*shakes her head*).
TOMAS: Then he won't be coming.
MÄRTA: Are you expecting him?
Tomas' head sinks deeply behind his arms. He doesn't answer, but after

a while she hears his voice, edgy and embittered. Again and again he interrupts himself, his head sinks even deeper.

TOMAS: I had just a faint—a faint hope he'd come—in spite of everything. That everything wouldn't turn out to be illusions, dreams, lies.

Immediately she is with him. Silencing him, she presses his head hard against her flat thin breast, the hard buttons of her woollen cardigan. He begins to cough. She frees him, sits down beside him in the pew.

TOMAS: I've got to get ready. Service in Frostnäs church at three.

MÄRTA: I'll come with you.

TOMAS: No.

Tomas gets up and dries his face and eyes. Blows his nose. Märta moves away from him. The door to the porch opens and the old woman from Hol is standing there, confused and trembling.

THE WOMAN: I saw the Vicar's car was still here, so I've come; Fredriksson's boys found him.

TOMAS *(distraught)*: Yes.

THE WOMAN: Just down the hill.

She points with her gloved finger, anxiously looking at Tomas.

TOMAS: Found him? Was he dead?

THE WOMAN: Jonas Persson. *(Nods)* He's shot himself through the head with his shotgun. The police superintendent has just arrived, he's taking it all down. The boys ran and fetched him. I met them on my way here. They were terrified.

Without replying Tomas goes into the vestry, flings his scarf round his neck, kicks off his shoes and pulls his boots on. Then he shuts his brief-case and pulls on his leather gloves.

Märta is standing in the sacristy doorway.

He goes out into the church, past Märta, past the old woman, out of the great door, down toward his car.

The sun casts his long shadow in the snow.

III

The little parking place in front of the churchyard gate is freezing in the shade. He unlocks his car, slips inside, into its cold raw air. Starts the motor, lets it run a few moments, sets the windshield wipers going. With a laborious squeaking noise they wipe away the snow which has fallen thickly on the windshield. As he lets in the clutch, the wheels skid a moment or two; but the old car is heavy and reluctantly lumbers off down the hill, toward the main road.

The police car, with engine purring, stands just before the turning to the jetty. The superintendent and another man are bending over a body stretched out in the snow. It has half slid down into the ditch. A short way off Fredriksson's boys, frozen into immobility, noses running and woollen caps pulled down over their eyes, stand staring, frightened, curious. One of them has a pair of ski sticks under his arm.

Jonas is lying face downwards, the snow round his head has partly melted. Elsewhere it is deep red. His shotgun is lying in the ditch. One hand is outstretched.

The superintendent pays his formal respects to the vicar. Of course, yes, it's suicide; no question about that. No, not an accident. Unthinkable. Persson was an experienced huntsman, he knew how to handle firearms. Suicide, certainly. For the last half year he'd been brooding. Only the other day the superintendent had spoken to Söderberg down at the boatyard, only a couple of days ago they'd been talking about Jonas and telling themselves how much he'd changed of late. Introverted and brooding, as he'd said. So it was suicide, no question. Even so, he must be taken to the infirmary, for the death certificate. The Fribergs have a van, we can take the corpse there in it.

The stranger offers to go down to Friberg to ask if they can borrow the van. The superintendent and Tomas move the dead man to the edge of the wood, behind the bushes; from the trunk of his car he takes out a stained tarpaulin and lays it over the corpse. He throws the shotgun into the back seat. With avuncular dignity he turns to the little boys, speaking to them with friendly authority.

SUPERINTENDENT: Come on now, boys, let's go.

Fredriksson's boys thaw out of their frozen posture, and make off for the main road. The older drags his ski-sticks after him.

SUPERINTENDENT: If you'll keep an eye on things a few minutes, I'll just run home and ring the infirmary and the police in town. There's always such a hell of a lot of formalities nowadays.

TOMAS: Go ahead, I'll wait.

SUPERINTENDENT: If Friberg gets here before me, just load it on and get going. Tell him that, will you, from me. Thanks.

Tomas nods, steps over the ditch and goes up to the dead man. Now they've all gone. He is alone with Jonas.
The sun goes down; for a while it had shone on the edges of the cloud, causing them to glow; now the afternoon turns greyly into night. The pine trees are soughing and once again the snow begins to fall, thick and ceaseless.
Complete stillness.
Someone is coming along the road. It is Märta, approaching with long strides, her hands thrust deeply down into her sheepskin jacket. She catches sight of Tomas, comes to a halt at the edge of the ditch.
TOMAS: Sit in the car for the moment.
She hesitates, but obeys. After a short wait the engine of a car is heard and Friberg's van comes slowly clambering up the slope. The men help each other to lift the body into the van.
TOMAS: Tell the superintendent I'll drive over to Mrs. Persson.
The men nod and take their leave.
Tomas gets into his car and starts it up.
TOMAS: You forgot the coffee basket in the church.
MÄRTA: I can get it tomorrow.
After a few minutes' drive they stop below the school house, a red-painted wooden building with two schoolrooms on the ground floor and the teacher's apartment on the first floor. In the yard, which is joined to the road by a short stretch of driveway, stands a huge linden tree. It provides accommodation for a couple of crows' nests. The dark birds are flying to and fro in its branches.
MÄRTA: Good-bye, then, Tomas.
TOMAS: Good-bye.
Silence.
MÄRTA: Maybe I'll hear from you some time this week.
TOMAS: Have you got such a thing as a couple of aspirin?
MÄRTA: Of course. I've got some cough mixture, too.
TOMAS: Maybe that'd be good.
MÄRTA: Come in with me.
TOMAS: But your aunt is there, isn't she?
MÄRTA: You can wait in the classroom while I go up and fetch it. It won't take a moment.
They get out of the car after Tomas has driven it in to the school drive, Märta's bicycle is standing, rather the worse for snow, in the yard. She picks it up and carries it into the porch.
On the right lies a classroom, still used by its six pupils. It is a big

dilapidated room, worn by the years. In one corner is a radio and on the longer wall, opposite the windows, the children have mounted an exhibition of their paintings and drawings.

Tomas drops on to one of the school benches. Märta goes upstairs and is heard speaking to her aunt about the cake. Suddenly the crows screech, and he looks out of the window. A boy is coming across the yard, followed by a huge Alsatian, which dashes after one of the irritating crows. Then there's a rumbling in the porch. Dog and boy come into the classroom. Tomas greets him; the boy, surprised and shy, replies. The dog sniffs suspiciously at the vicar's boots, but decides to accept him and goes out into the entrance hall.

TOMAS: Who's son are you?

BOY: Strand's.

TOMAS: How old are you?

BOY: Ten.

TOMAS: What are you doing in here on a Sunday?

BOY: Forgot something in my desk.

TOMAS: What's the dog's name?

BOY: Jim.

TOMAS: Is he yours?

BOY: No.

TOMAS: Then he's your older brother's? The one who's being confirmed this year!

BOY: Yes.

TOMAS: Are you going to come to confirmation class?

BOY: No.

TOMAS: Oh, why not?

BOY (*embarrassed*): Don't know.

The boy, who has picked a lurid comic out of his desk and is standing in front of Tomas, looking out of the window, twists and scrapes his snow-covered boot.

TOMAS: Does your brother think the classes are boring?

BOY: Mm. I dunno.

TOMAS: What are you going to be when you grow up?

The boy shifts his glance and looks Tomas straight between the eyes with an expression of indulgent disdain.

BOY: Spaceman.

TOMAS (*suddenly smiles*): Sure. I understand. Good-bye, then.

The boy, polite but silent, bows, calls his dog. At the same moment Märta comes downstairs. In her hand she is carrying a tray with a glass, a bottle, a spoon, and packets of powder.

MÄRTA: Good afternoon, Johan. What are you doing here?
BOY (*patiently*): Came to get something I forgot in my desk.

He shows his comic. Märta asks him about someone called Pelle. The boy says Pelle is much better and on his feet since Friday. Maybe he'll be coming to school in the middle of the week. Märta asks Johan to give her regards to his parents. He promises to do this. In the end, with Jim, who wags his tail at the teacher, he goes off.

Märta comes in and sits down at the desk opposite Tomas. She puts aside the tray and pours out some cough medicine into a large spoon. He swallows it obediently, makes a face, and takes the glass of water.

MÄRTA: Be careful how you drink it. It's hot. It's really for gargling with. You put these pills in and they dissolve. I got them from Aunt. She says they're excellent pills.

TOMAS: No thanks.

MÄRTA: But . . . but Aunt says she's always getting sore throats and that these pills help almost at once.

TOMAS: No thanks.

MÄRTA: As you like. Anyway, here are your aspirins. Shall I get you a glass of water to swallow them with?

TOMAS: No thanks. No need.

MÄRTA: How unfriendly you sound.

TOMAS (*says nothing, swallows the tablets*).

MARTA: Sometimes . . .

TOMAS (*looks at her*).

MÄRTA: Sometimes you sound almost as if you hated me.

TOMAS (*silent, swallows*).

The silence swells to an explosion. She proffers him the packet of tablets, but he doesn't see it.

MÄRTA (*in a low voice*): You can take the whole packet if you like. Aunt has brought a whole chemist's shop with her.

Unsure of herself, she smiles again. Tomas begins to wind his scarf round his neck and button up his coat.

MÄRTA: Can't I come with you to Frostnäs?

TOMAS: I've got to go to the Perssons' first.

MÄRTA: I can wait in the car.

TOMAS: But your aunt has baked a cake.

MÄRTA (*sadly*): Tomas.

TOMAS: I want to be left in peace.

MÄRTA: Do you want to get rid of me?

92

TOMAS (*angrily*): No, not that. Märta, not just now. Not just now. For God's sake, I can't bear it, not just now.

MÄRTA: Why do you want to get rid of me?

Tomas makes a gesture of extreme weariness. He had half risen but now he sits down again and passes his hands over his face.

MÄRTA: Tomas, dearest beloved Tomas, you're getting old. You're dissatisfied with your life, with everything, most of all with yourself. And here am I, throwing myself in your arms. It doesn't make sense with the rest of the picture.

She checks herself. Tomas looks up and gives a rather cruel smile, but says nothing.

MÄRTA (*in a low voice*): Or does it make all too good sense?

TOMAS: You can see for yourself.

MÄRTA (*hastily*): I know, you have your dreams, dearest Tomas. And I don't bother about them. Sometimes I've even rather despised them. (*Nods*) Yes. I could have been kinder.

TOMAS: Those are just trivialities, Märta.

MÄRTA: Not so trivial. You've been unlucky, really. I know I'm an authoritarian, a terrible one for taking charge of others. Yes. (*Pause*) Don't contradict me.

TOMAS: Will you listen to me a moment?

MÄRTA: I'm sorry. I do all the talking.

TOMAS: I feel humiliated by all this gossip. Once no one cared what the clergyman thought. He was just a sort of necessary piece of equipment, one of the fittings, though no one really knew what use he was. Then the rumours began, about you and me. A terrible whispering and muttering. Imagine it, the vicar. My word, the vicar isn't all he ought to be, either. Well you know how they talk.

MÄRTA: Is *that* your reason?

TOMAS: You needn't sound so scornful.

MÄRTA: Well, then marry me.

TOMAS: No. (*Shakes his head*) No. (*Pause*)

MÄRTA: Tomas, my dear, it's so hard to plead one's own cause.

TOMAS: Yes, it's hard.

MÄRTA: You can't, you mustn't push me away. It's incomprehensible how you can be so blind.

TOMAS: Märta, please. Don't get hysterical.

MÄRTA: That's what you always say when you see me crying. And of course, I am a little hysterical, I suppose.

TOMAS: Märta, calm down. Think if your aunt hears us.

MÄRTA: I can't help it, can I, if the tears come? You can go on talking as usual, I can hear every word you say.

They watch each other, waiting; suddenly the boil of silence bursts, and the poison comes pouring out.

TOMAS (*calmly*): I thought I'd figured out a good reason. I mean all that about the vicar's reputation. Surely she'll understand that, I thought.

MÄRTA (*stares at him*).

TOMAS: But you waved it away, that reason, and I understand you. After all, it's a lie.

MÄRTA (*troubled*).

TOMAS: The reason, the one that matters, is that I don't want you.

MÄRTA (*motionless, long silence*).

TOMAS: Do you hear what I'm saying?

MÄRTA (*quiet*): Of course I can hear what you're saying.

TOMAS: I'm tired of your loving care, your fussing over me, your good advice, your little candlesticks and table-runners. I'm fed up with your short-sightedness and your clumsy hands, your anxiousness and your timid ways when we make love. You force me to occupy myself with your physical condition, your bad stomach, your eczemas, your periods, your frostbitten cheek. Once and for all I must get out of all this rubbish, this junkheap of idiotic circumstances. I'm sick and tired of the whole thing, of everything to do with you.

MÄRTA: Why haven't you told me this before?

TOMAS: For a simple reason. I'm well brought up. From birth I've been taught to regard women as beings of a higher order, admirable creatures, unimpeachable martyrs.

MÄRTA (*quietly*): And your wife?

TOMAS: I loved her! D'you hear that? I loved her! But I don't love you. Because I loved my wife. And when she died, so did I. And it's a matter of complete indifference to me whether life goes on, or what happens to me. D'you understand what I'm saying! I loved her and she was everything you can never be, and which you're always trying to be. The way you mimic her behaviour is just an ugly parody.

MÄRTA (*calm*): I didn't even know her.

TOMAS: I'd better be going. (*With dry despair*) I'd better be going before I talk worse nonsense.

MÄRTA: Is there any worse?

TOMAS (*doesn't answer*).

MÄRTA (*takes off her glasses*).

TOMAS: Stop rubbing your eyes like that.

MÄRTA: Forgive me.

TOMAS: Go on. Look. I can stand it.

MÄRTA (*a faint smile*): I can hardly see you without my glasses. You're all fuzzy and your face is just a white blob—you're not really real.

She sits pondering, fingers her glasses, her head is bowed, her broad shoulders hunched.

MÄRTA (*to herself*): I understand. I've done the wrong thing. From the beginning.

Tomas fiddles with his glass, spins it round in his hand, lifts it up and raises it to his lips, sets it down again.

TOMAS (*pained*): I must go now. I've got to talk to Mrs. Persson.

MÄRTA: No, I've done wrong. Every time I've felt hatred for you I've made an effort to turn it into pity. (*Looks at him*) I've been sorry for you. I've got so used to being sorry for you, I can't even hate you.

She smiles, apologetically—her wry ironical smile. He throws her a brief glance. The hunched shoulders, the bowed head, the large motionless hands, the look in her eye, suddenly defenseless, burning, the lobes of her ears which stick out from beneath her thin, uncombed hair.

MÄRTA: What'll become of you—without me?

TOMAS: Oh!

A disdainful gesture. He bites his lip. A heavy disgust is working itself up through his entrails, into his head. It attacks him like a sort of seasickness, he yawns convulsively.

MÄRTA (*distraught*): Oh no, you won't be able to manage. You'll go under, dearest Tomas. Nothing can save you. You'll hate the life out of yourself.

TOMAS: Why can't you be quiet! Can't you leave me in peace? Why can't you shut up!

He gets up and goes toward the door, she remains seated in the same hunched posture. As he comes out into the hall he turns:

TOMAS: Want to come to Frostnäs with me? (*Pause*) I'll try not to be nasty.

She looks up. Her face wears a shut-in, stern expression.
MÄRTA (*stiffly*): Will you, really? Or is it just that some new
fright's flown into you?
TOMAS: Do as you like; but I'm asking you to come.
MÄRTA: Of course. Naturally I'll come. I haven't any choice,
have I?
*She gathers together the objects on the little tray, carries it out into the
hallway, goes a few steps up the stairs, tightening the belt of her sheepskin
coat. Tomas goes out.*
MÄRTA (*calls*): Aunt! I'll be home at six. D'you hear?—She must
be asleep, I must go up and see she hasn't left something on
the stove.
*She fetches the tray, runs up the stairs and disappears into the flat above.
Tomas walks down towards his car. All trace of earlier footsteps is
already hidden beneath the snow. He gets into the car, starts the engine.
An old man is coming along the road. He is leading a big black horse on
a halter. They slip and struggle on the slushy slope. As he passes the car,
the man touches his cap to the vicar.*
Then Märta comes running.
MÄRTA: I've brought the tablets.
*Tomas doesn't bother to answer. With an impatient jerk he slams the door
shut. Stuffs the pillbox into his pocket and makes himself comfortable.*
*They drive down the road to the fisherman's house. The windshield mists
over. Märta wipes it off with her glove. They meet a car with its head-
lights on. Tomas switches on the parking lights.*
*The motor hums monotonously, its sound damped by snow, now and then
the tires hiss as they pass through a stretch of wet snow.*
*The road goes straight through the forest, sloping gently towards the sea. In
among the trees it is night.*
Both sit silent, sunk in their own thoughts.
*Jonas Persson's house is an old summer villa, surrounded by a dilapidated
orchard. Below the house, high sand-dunes, crowned by a sparse copse of
pines. The sea, still not ice-bound, is grey-black, dully mumbling in the
dusk.*
*A paraffin lamp is shining in the kitchen, and Tomas can see Mrs. Persson
moving about between her stove and kichen table by the window. The
children are eating. The oldest daughter, a plump motherly thirteen-year-
old, has the youngest child on her knee and is patiently feeding it.*
*The boy is sitting at the end of the table with his long thin neck against the
window. Round his neck he has wound a stocking. At the other end of the*

table, two plates, glasses, a beer bottle and knives and forks. Mrs.Persson is just about to sit down beside her oldest daughter—when she catches sight of Tomas out on the porch.

She says something to the thirteen-year-old, goes into the hallway and opens the door. Tomas steps inside. A smell of cauliflower and moldy fruit, stored through the winter, hits him.

The last remnants of the afternoon light are not strong enough to light up the oblong room with its bulging wallpaper and dirty stairs. The woman's face is big and blurred, her eyes black hollows.

She stands with her hand on the doorknob, swollen and sunken. Her hair hangs down around her brow.

TOMAS: Your husband is dead, Mrs. Persson. They've driven him to the infirmary, but there's nothing to be done. He shot himself.

Her hand lets go of the doorknob and she sits down on the stair, pulls down her skirt over her knees and swollen legs. Her hands keep a firm grasp on the hem of her skirt.

MRS. PERSSON: So I'm alone then.

Tomas sits down on a stool. He clasps his hands on his knee, mostly out of habit. They sit silent.

TOMAS: Shall we read something out of the Bible together?

MRS. PERSSON: No, no thanks.

TOMAS (*nods*).

MRS. PERSSON: I'll tell the children.

She grasps the banister rail and pulls herself up, offering her hand to Tomas.

TOMAS: If there's anything I can do for you, I'm home all the evening. I mean if . . .

MRS. PERSSON: Yes, thank you. I'll look in during the week. Of course, we'll have to discuss the funeral.

Tomas lets go of her hand. He stands there, clumsy, uncertain.

TOMAS: I spoke to him, but there was so little I could do.

She stares the vicar straight in the face, as if her thoughts are already far away, Then, as if suddenly aware again of his presence, nods.

MRS. PERSSON: I'm sure you did what you could, sir.

Again Tomas offers his hand, but Mrs.Persson doesn't see it. She goes into the kitchen, shuts the door.

As Tomas comes out into the porch he turns round and looks into the kitchen. Mrs.Persson is standing leaning against the table, talking to her children, turning mostly to the boy. The older ones are listening attentively, while the littlest one has taken a spoon and stuck it deep into her mouth and is eagerly chewing it.

He goes down the dusky steps from the porch. Jonas' dog appears out of the darkness, an old Lapp dog; first he growls, warningly, then goes up to Tomas and suspiciously sniffs at him. Then vanishes round the corner of the house.

The road follows the sea. It's lighter here and on the horizon to the southward are two golden colored streaks of cloud, bluish toward their edges. Somewhere beyond the islands a lighthouse flashes and the stony shore is already covered with ice. The water is a toneless blackness, whitened by breakers over the shallow spits.

MÄRTA: I'll drive if you're tired.

TOMAS: No thanks.

MÄRTA: Did you talk to her?

TOMAS (*nods*).

The road turns inland. At the level crossing, just before Frostnäs station, the booms come down, the railway bell clangs and the stop light burns. Tomas brakes and switches off the engine. From far off the train can be heard approaching.

THOMAS: One evening when I was a boy I woke up in a terrible state of fright. The train shrieked down at the corner, you remember we lived in the old vicarage by the bridge. It was an early spring evening with a strange wild light over the ice and the forest. I got out of bed, ran round all the rooms looking for Father. But the house was empty. I shouted and screamed, but no one answered. So I dressed as well as I could and ran down to the shore, all the time screaming and crying for Father.

In a cloud of steam and snow flurries, the train rolls by with a majestic roar. Its buffers and couplings rattle, and the brakes and axles whine. The carriages lean over and shake as they go round the curve, the points crash and the train comes squealing and panting to a halt at Frostnäs station.

TOMAS: I'd been left without Father and Mother in a completely dead world. I was sick with terror. Father sat up and watched over me all night.

MÄRTA (*absent-mindedly*):   What a nice father!

TOMAS: Father and Mother wanted me to become a parson (*pause*) and I did as they wished.

Hesitantly, the booms go up; their journey continues, up towards the church, which lies on the other side of the hamlet.

IV

*On the little street with its four shops a few half-grown boys are standing
in a group. With great effort two little girls are dragging a third along
on a sled. As its runners cut through the thin blanket of snow they
laugh gaily. Through the snow-mist lights can be seen shining from a
few windows.*

*Down at the station the train starts moving, filling the air with smoke
and furious snortings.*

*The car swings up the side-road toward the church, which lies at the end
of an avenue of ancient elms. The building is of fairly recent date, from
the beginning of the nineteenth century, in the strict light style of that age,
with a pulpit and altar piece in late rococo.*

*The snow has ceased falling but the cold has come down, with windy
gusts and frozen fog.*

*Tomas drives round the church and stops behind it. In a farm across the
road a dog barks insistently. Then the two church bells begin tolling for
the service, their roar washing away all other sounds. Tomas and Märta
remain seated a moment in the car, listening.*

MÄRTA: Think of the summertime, those bells, when the sun
burns on the fjord. And the birch woods. The smell of
jasmine. "Now cometh lovely summer with charms and
sweet desires . . ."

*Tomas turns his head and looks at her. She becomes shy and silent. Tomas
reaches over to the back seat for his brief-case.*

*He is overcome by a bad attack of coughing and has to support himself
against the back of the front seat.*

Meanwhile Algot Frövik is lighting the lamps in the chancel.

*When Tomas and Märta step into the dark church, lit only at the altar,
he rushes past them, greeting them politely but hurriedly, to switch off the
electric switch to the church bells. Having done this he shakes his head and
mumbles to himself.*

ALGOT: What a nuisance, they rang twenty seconds too long.
A nuisance but there is an explanation. I've put new candles
in the altar candlesticks. I usually have time to switch on
the bells, go up and light the candles and be back in good
time to switch off again. Today I made a mess of it. A
regrettable error. But the candles were new and hard to
light! Presumably some fault from the factory. It's also

99

conceivable my wretched body takes more and more time to carry out the simplest functions. But it's all one; if I may say so.

During his long speech they have reached the sanctuary. Algot switches on the electric light under the organ gallery.

ALGOT: I always let the temple repose in half darkness until just before the bells start. According to my way of seeing it, the electric lights disturb our spirit of reverence before the commencement of a service. Isn't that so, Vicar? Isn't that so, Miss Lundberg?

With surprising swiftness Algot has brought out and hung up the cope and switched on the electric central heating radiator in the sacristy.

At the same time he opens the book of notices and lays it on the table before Tomas, who has sat down to take off his boots.

TOMAS: And how are you, Mr.Frövik?

ALGOT: No use complaining, Vicar. My aches don't get any better in such weather, of course. But I'm on my legs.

TOMAS: And at home?

ALGOT: Thank you, thank you. My old woman's got a job in the jam factory and I do the housekeeping. So we're better off every day. And how are you, Vicar? Not too good, I fancy?

TOMAS: You wanted to talk to me this morning.

ALGOT: Yes, as a matter of fact it was urgent.

TOMAS: Well?

ALGOT: Once, when I complained about my pains keeping me awake at night, you suggested I should read something to distract my thoughts.

TOMAS: I remember.

ALGOT: I began with the gospels. Real sleeping tablets, they were, if I may say so!

TOMAS (*smiles*): Really?

ALGOT: In between whiles, that is. In between whiles. Now I've got as far as the story of Christ's passion. And that's given me something to think about. So I thought, I'd better have a word about this with Rev. Ericsson.

Algot twists on his chair so as to find a more comfortable posture, and swings up one arm so that his hand rests against the table.

ALGOT (*ready to burst*): Christ's passion, Vicar. It's incorrect to think of it as Christ's passion, isn't that so?

100

TOMAS: What do you mean?

ALGOT: We think too much about the actual torture, so to speak. But that can't have been so bad. Well, excuse me, it sounds a bit presumptuous, of course, but physically, if I may say so without being too assuming, I must have suffered, so to speak, at least as much as ever Christ did. Besides which, his torments were rather brief. About four hours or so?

TOMAS (*looks at Algot*).

ALGOT: I thought I saw a much greater suffering behind the physical one.

TOMAS: Oh, did you?

ALGOT: Maybe I've got it all wrong in some way. (*Silent; takes up a new position*) But think of Gethsemane, Vicar. All his disciples asleep. They hadn't understood a thing, not the last supper, nothing. And then when the servants of the law arrived, off they ran. And then Peter, who denied him. For three years Christ had been talking to these disciples, Vicar, day in day out they'd lived together. And they'd quite simply not grasped what he meant. Not a word. They abandoned him, the whole lot of them. And he was left alone. (*Passionately*) Vicar, that must have been a terrible suffering! To understand that no one has understood you. To be abandoned when one really needs someone to rely on. A terrible suffering.

TOMAS (*after a pause*): Yes. Obviously.

ALGOT: Well. But that wasn't the worst thing, even so! When Christ had been nailed up on the cross and hung there in his torments, he cried out: "God, my God, why hast thou forsaken me." He cried out as loud as he possibly could. He thought his Father in Heaven had abandoned him. He believed everything he'd been preaching was a lie. The moments before he died, Christ was seized with a great doubt. Surely that must have been his most monstrous suffering of all? I mean God's silence. Isn't that true, Vicar?

TOMAS: Yes, yes. (*Nods, averting his face*).

Märta, who has been standing in the door listening to Algot's worried excogitations, goes down into the church and sits down in a pew to one side. She can hear voices in there, in the sacristy. Tomas coughs. Algot is glimpsed for a moment, as if looking for something. Then he's gone again.

101

Märta looks at her wrist watch. It shows ten minutes to three. No church-
goer has yet shown up.
Noise is heard at the entrance. The door is opened and Fredrik Blom, the
organist, hurries up the aisle to the sanctuary. He catches sight of Märta,
waves, comes up to her, shakes her by the hand, breathes on her.

BLOM: Mark my words, there'll be no service today. Not a
churchgoer, not a soul. Who goes to the house of the Lord
in such weather? You don't count. You belong, so to speak,
in the sheep-pen.

MÄRTA: Is your wife here?

BLOM: Not her! She stayed behind at the christening. So I had
to get here as best I could.

A few veins swell in his fat face. Suddenly his chummy manner runs out
on him, his glance is sharply ill-natured.

BLOM: That vicar you're running after, Märta, he's not worth
much. Let me tell you. Oh yes, yes; yes, I know. Don't
contradict. You're on the slippery slope. You're taking what
you can get.

He laughs, but his glance is still jagged.

BLOM: For your own sake, Märta. You who can move, get out
as quick as you can. Everything here at Mittsunda and
Frostnäs is in the grip of death and decay. Look at me.
Remember the days when I used to arrange evenings of
organ music. On that old heap of junk. And had a real
choir. Concerts.

He passes the back of his hand over his mouth, leans close over her, fanning
her with his breath, nods in confirmation of his words.

BLOM: And the things Tomas achieved! The church, both this
one and the one at Mittsunda, had people in 'em, see? But
his wife was the end of him.

Märta, who has been paying no attention to his chatter, is suddenly all ears.

BLOM: Ah, that interested you, didn't it. Yes? his wife. A proper
woodlouse. When she really got seriously ill, no one believed
her. And then she died. That at least, I suppose, wasn't put
on. And Tomas, he's got about as much knowledge of human
nature as my old galoshes. He only had eyes for her. Lived
for her, he did. Loved her like a lunatic. She, who hadn't a
genuine feeling in her whole body, not an honest thought.
That's what you can call love, if you like! Jesus! But it put
an end to the vicar, it did. And now he's done for.

102

Blom leans even closer, he's almost in a good mood, lays a chubby hand on her shoulder.

BLOM: Listen, Märta. That's how it was with *that* love. *(Quotes)*: "God is love, and love is God. Love is the proof of God's existence. Love exists as something real in the world of men and women." I know the jargon, as you can hear. I've been an attentive listener to the vicar's outpourings—'Bye— *(laughs)* you old turtledove!

His evil mood has evaporated as quickly as it came, he goes a few steps away from her and scratches the back of his left hand.

BLOM: Get out while you can.

He opens his eyes wide, as if to see clearly. Goes into the sacristy, leaving Märta to her lonely thoughts.

Tomas coughs, his eyes are feverish and bloodshot, he is sitting leaning forward over the table, reading the draft of his sermon. Algot is soundlessly busy in some corner.

BLOM: Hello, you tubercular old wheezer. No thanks, I'm not shaking hands, certainly don't want to catch your influenza. Well, how's it to be? Service, or no service?

TOMAS: I don't feel too well.

BLOM: Florence Nightingale is sitting out there, waiting to look after you. Myself, I'd much appreciate an afternoon snooze. I'm playing this evening at the masonic lodge, see? What does Algot say?

ALGOT: Nothing.

BLOM: I'll go up to the organ. Algot can give me a sign when the bells stop.

Blom goes off. Tomas pours out a glass of water and takes two more of Märta's aspirin tablets.

Algot goes over to the door to look.

TOMAS: Well?

ALGOT *(sadly)*: No, only Miss Lundberg sitting out there. *(Apologetically)*. Well, of course, that's not to say "only".

TOMAS: What shall we do?

ALGOT: Don't ask me, Vicar. I can see well enough you're really bad, and we certainly won't be a crowd. But, well . . . don't ask me.

He looks at the floor and the wall, scratches some unevenness in the plaster with his fingernail, looks apologetically at his watch.

ALGOT: It's time to start the service bell. People usually stir their stumps when they hear it. I mean, if there's anyone coming up the road.

He hurries down the aisle and bows politely to Märta, who doesn't even look in his direction. Then the bells are set in motion, tolling out once again through the twilight and the icy wind.

Märta is overcome with violent emotion. To master an unusual and powerful shuddering she clasps her hands, presses her arms tightly against her sides, deeply bows her head.

MÄRTA (*slowly with pauses*): If I could only lead him out of his emptiness, away from his lie-god. If we could dare to show each other tenderness. If we could believe in a truth . . . If we could believe . . .

Tomas gets up out off his chair, stands shivering in the middle of the room. The service bell ends with a few resounding clangs. The twilight has begun to deepen into darkness. Algot peers in through the sacristy door.

TOMAS: Well?

ALGOT: Well, of course, Miss Lundberg's still there. And someone might still come in during the first hymn.

TOMAS (*looks at Algot*).

ALGOT: So. A service?

TOMAS (*nods*): Yes.

Algot looks at Tomas in surprise. Makes a sign to Blom on the organ gallery, who immediately intones a hurried prelude.

Algot steps into the church and sits down close to the aisle, supporting the organist's rather melodious bass with vague mumbling song.

During the hymn Tomas goes up to the altar, kneels, rises, turns a pale and anxiety-filled face to his congregation.

TOMAS: "Holy, holy, holy, Lord God Almighty. All the earth is full of his glory . . ."

THE SILENCE

Djursholm
March, 1962

The Silence

I

The night express.
The compartment windows are open but the draft presses against one's
face like a fever breath, provides no relief from the heat. A sooty curtain
flaps frantically.
Anna, sweating and half-comatose, has sunk down in her seat; her son
Johan, ten, leans against her body, asleep. The stinking, dusty plush seat
gives no comfort, her summer dress is crumpled and she sits with sweating
thighs wide apart.
Now and then she yawns, stares at the landscape's monstrous plains.
The lights in the compartment are out and in the remote distance the
dawn light reveals the outline of a jagged chain of hills.
In the other corner sits Ester. Apparently unaffected by the heat, she holds
herself upright, the palms of her hands rest on the cushions, her eyes are
closed. But her face is tormented and pale.
These three are alone in the compartment, which floats onward in the
silence of dawn.
The boy wakes up, wants something to drink. His mother gives him an
orange.
He gets up impatiently, goes out into the corridor; almost immediately
returns, stops and reads a printed notice affixed to the compartment door.
Asks Ester what it says. She shakes her head, doesn't know.
Obstinately the boy persists, spelling it out: NITSEL STANT NJON
PALIK. *Anna tells him to sit down, or lie down and try to sleep. He*
clambers up onto the seat, lays his head against her knee.
Gently, she slips a cushion under his head. The train comes uncertainly
to a halt.
There is no station, no signal, no one is walking about or meeting anyone.
The plains are utterly still, unmoving. In the next compartment someone
moves about and speaks indistinctly, in a low vague voice.
Ester turns her face to the light of the window pane with its limp curtain.
She is shaken by repressed coughing, puts the palm of her hand to her
mouth; moans, shakes her head, bends her head down towards her knees.

Her mouth opens and a stream of blood and froth runs over her legs and down to the floor.

Anna tries to hold her head, but she hits out at her hands and throws herself backwards against the wall, choking.

The boy has sat up. He stares at her, more amazed than terrified.

Ester calms down, gets her breath back. She passes her hand over her face and mechanically begins wiping the blood off her skirt with her handkerchief.

But her respite is only brief. A new wave of cramps convulses her body, she gets up and staggers to the window. Anna throws her arms round her sister's waist to support her.

As suddenly as it came, the attack is over.

She lies down and closes her eyes. Anna sits at her side, wiping her chin and mouth. Slowly the train begins to move again.

The boy stands at the window, trying not to notice the flecks of blood on the glass.

The sun rises over the hills, throwing a long shadow over the plain's scorched grasses and striking his tired eyes with its fierce light. A stench of sweat, dust and hot iron stings his nose.

But there is also another odour, dark and sweet, which passes its cold finger through the lining of his stomach. The curtain flaps against the wall, tinged by the morning light.

He goes out into the corridor. Two elderly gentlemen in uniform are asleep in the neighboring compartment. Each lies on one of the seats, mouth open, though not snoring. On the little table by the window stand two half-empty beer bottles and a tall smoke-spiral rises from a cigarette in the ashtray.

The conductor comes. He throws a hasty glance into the women's compartment, pauses, opens the door. Johan hears him speaking to his mother; mumbling, incomprehensible. Now and then Ester says something.

ESTER: It's nothing—No, I don't want to go into hospital. Just rest a day at a hotel.

The conductor, serious, shakes his head, opens his timetable and puts his thumbnail on a typewritten figure, then shakes his head again, shows his wrist watch.

The mother looks at Ester, uncertain what to do. They mumble something to each other. Johan leaves them. He feels safer by the sleeping uniforms.

In the corridor there is a wooden folding seat. He sits on it with bowed back, resting his chin on the window ledge.

The wheels clatter over the points, rails leap out from one another, a

108

marshalling yard comes into view: a stationary freight train, an iron bridge over the dark green of a squirting waterfall.
Yet another goods train, laden with guns, armored cars and soldiers.
A clump of grey-black houses with dark window openings, factory walls, backyards, rusting trollies: the marshalling yard grows wider, curves and swells majestically. A church tower throws its shadow, like a bar, across the rails; signals flip past, then a tunnel with flashing lights.
On the other side of the tunnel the sunlight hits him full in the face. A whirling spiral of sand arises around the creaking, braking carriage. Out of the cloud rises a great wall.
On it, written in huge green letters on a yellow background the words: ARKIN STAJK. A hand holds a long black cigar.
The loudspeaker in the depths of the corridor begins crackling and a voice speaks quickly but clearly: TIMOKAN RETJE FEL SIS TIMOKAN RETJE FEL SIS.

II

Johan is standing at the hotel room window, looking down into the street. Quite narrow, the street leads up from the main road toward a brick church surrounded by tall iron railings.
The pavements are full of people moving incessantly in either direction, many are walking out in the road, of which the right side is blocked by a long row of parked cars.
The sunshine slashes a deep chasm between the fronts of the tall, dirty grey-white houses.
Opposite the hotel's stately turn-of-the-century façade there is a bar; a deep cave thrust into the body of the house. A glimpse of a counter and tables; people moving in and out, like bees in a hive.
Beside the bar is a movie theater. It has just opened for the day's showings and its manager is taking down the grill. Its advertising panels are filled with garish mountains of womanhood. A sharp glimmer of neon struggles, not unsuccessfully, against the morning light, in bold curves etching out the name of the theater.
By the railings of the brick church stands a newspaper stand, two vendors are antiphonally shouting out the black and red headlines of the news banners.
These are the only sounds that disturb the oppressive silence.
Down in the canyon of the street swarms of people move swiftly and

109

silently. No honking horns, no clatter of heels or sudden laughter, no music out of the grotto of the bar. Only two hoarse voices at the corner of the street, one shrill, shrieking; the other hoarse, penetrating.

Anna tells Johan to shut the window. He obeys at once, climbing down from his chair. She comes up to him from behind and draws the transparent white curtain. She has taken off her travelling dress and is wearing a green silk housecoat. As she leans forward to fix the window he is strongly aware of her body's perfume. Playfully, he seizes her belt and checks her as she turns back into the room. She gives a little irritated smile smoothing his hair with her broad damp hand.

Johan sits down on the floor and draws his knees up under his chin, observing his mother, particularly her naked feet with their red lacquered toenails and strong high insteps. They move as it were of their own accord, steering themselves to and fro across the great worn carpet.

Anna catches sight of him in the cupboard mirror.

ANNA: What are you looking at?

JOHAN: I'm looking at your feet.

ANNA: Oh? Why?

JOHAN: They're walking about with you, all by themselves.

His mother goes into the next room, also a very large double room, elegant in the same old-fashioned turn-of-the-century style.

Ester has already gone to bed, her eyes are closed and her face is turned toward the window.

ANNA: Shouldn't we try and get a doctor, even so?

ESTER (*shakes her head*).

ANNA: D'you feel cold?

ESTER: A little.

ANNA: It's dreadfully hot.

ESTER: If I can only get some rest we'll go on tomorrow. On Monday we'll be home.

ANNA (*sighs*):   That'll be good.

ESTER (*smiles*):   I know you think so.

Indecisively Anna goes over to the window, as if wishing to open it.

ESTER: Is the air bad in here?

ANNA: Rather.

ESTER: Very well, open the window.

Anna opens the window, and then goes back to her own room. Johan is still sitting hunched on the floor, pondering.

ANNA: May I shut the door?

ESTER: Of course.

110

Anna shuts the door, searches in her handbag awhile and brings out a transparent box of multicolored bath salts.
She goes into the bathroom. Johan follows slowly after. She takes off her house coat, feels the temperature of the water, throws in the bath-capsules. She gets into the large, white bath.

JOHAN: You look nice with your hair like that.

Anna has tied a ribbon in her hair, baring her neck.

ANNA: Come and scrub my back.

The mother takes hold of the edges of the bath, sinking her head between her arms. He lays one hand on her shoulder and rests his head on her back.

ANNA: Hurry up now.

His mother's voice is faintly hostile. He is seized with a violent desire to cry, but controls himself. After he has scrubbed away awhile in silence, she takes the soap out of his hand.

ANNA: That's enough, go into the room till I tell you. We'll take an afternoon nap.

As always, he obeys. With a sigh he leaves her; sits down on one of the beds, which has been made up with huge bolsters. Flinging himself down on his back, he puts his feet up on the iron bedstead.
On either side of his face the bolster raises its white mountains. Lifting his arm he transforms his forefinger into a jet aircraft, which rushes roaring over the endless snowy landscape.
His mother comes in. She has put her shimmering green house coat on again.

ANNA: Take off your shirt and trousers.

He does so. His mother lets down the sunblinds, and the room is filled with a dark-grey twilight.
She fetches a bottle, pours some of the contents into the palm of her hand and bathes her face and shoulders. Stretching out her hands toward Johan, she wipes his forehead and neck with the cool, scented fluid.
Silent and solemn, lulled by his mother's perfumes, he sinks down into the bolsters' embrace. Almost immediately he drops off to sleep.
Ester tries to read, but cannot collect her thoughts. To calm herself she has smoked several cigarettes, but the smoke only makes her giddy and sets her coughing. A dull distant pain, threatening.
She pours herself out a big glass of cognac and gulps it down. An agree-able drowsiness spreads through her body. At last warmth returns, her anxiety dissipates, the pain grows less. In a better mood, she laughs at herself.

For a little while she has no difficulty in reading; but then the letters begin changing places and she finds it hard to follow the lines.

She throws the book on to the floor, gets out of bed. Opens the door to the other room.

Anna is lying face down, her nose deeply buried in her pillow, her rich hair an untidy mass over her face.

In the other bed Johan is asleep, his arms above his head and hands half-clenched like an infant's.

For a long while she contemplates the sleepers. Then she closes the door again and goes back to her own room. Stands at the window and looks down. Now the street is almost empty.

The sun scorches on the wall of the house opposite. The bar-owner is unrolling his big sun-awning.

A scraggy horse comes by, dragging a heavy load of old furniture and household goods.

Bar-owner and wagoner exchange a few words, the wagon halts and the driver disappears under the protective awning.

The horse stands with bowed head, its ribbed sides panting.

Ester pours out more cognac, talks a little to herself. On an impulse she rings the bedside bell. Quick footsteps in the corridor. A discreet knock at the door. Ester says 'yes' and the floor waiter appears. He is an elderly gentleman in an immaculate, if rather worn, suit of tails. His face is extraordinarily wrinkled. His hair is faded and dyed. His eyes hide behind thick black horn-rimmed glasses. His expression is serious, attentive.

Ester tries to speak to him in English, German, French, but he only shakes his head apologetically. She hands him the empty cognac glass and makes signs that she wants another. He smiles. It is a friendly smile, almost gay, which transforms his serious, impersonal features.

He goes out. Ester throws herself down in a chair and tries another cigarette. It goes more easily now, is almost pleasant. She draws a deep breath. Her feelings of sensuous pleasure and high spirits are not dissipated. Now she feels well and calm.

When the waiter comes back with a new bottle of cognac on a silver tray, Ester points to the other armchair by the little table. With a smile the waiter declines, and opens the bottle.

He fills a beautifully rounded, antique brandy glass, the sort which preserves the aroma, and with a politely expectant air presents both tray and glass.

Ester sniffs at the drink, gives an appreciative smile, sips it, and smiles

112

again. Offers him a cigarette. Apologetically, the waiter declines, makes as if to go.
Ester restrains him, points at her hand. He names the word in his own language.
She takes out a pen and on a block of yellowing paper writes down the word as she understands it.
The old man carefully examines what she has written, changes a few letters, shows her his correction and repeats the word slowly and clearly. He bows his appreciation. Suddenly he is troubled, points to the door, mimes his own swiftly running flat feet, gives himself a gentle smack in the face, and is gone.
Ester repeats the word: Hand, KASI. She reaches for her diary and writes the word in capitals on a fresh page. Then she yawns and gets up unsteadily, stubs her cigarette and sinks down on the bed, sitting there in her blue pyjamas, drunk and fearless.
Suddenly an air-raid siren wails out over the roofs of the houses, ripping up the compact sunburned silence with its short rhythmic howls. Then, as abruptly as it began, it stops. The stillness is even more compact and tangible.
Ester thrusts her hand inside her jacket and passes it over her breasts, cups one breast in the hollow of her hand, lies down cautiously, raises her knees and thrusts her other hand under the fabric of her pyjama pants.
A drowsy feeling of security comes over her, she wets her lips, presses her head back in the soft pillow. A few moments she lies still, panting, coughs slightly, stretches herself out and closes her eyes.
She rests, as if in tepid water. In soft, short spasms sleep approaches.

III

The boy wakes up to the howls of the siren, sits up in bed. He is completely rested, wholly content. His mother is sleeping deeply, motionless. Johan gives a sigh. It is by no means a miserable one, rather a sigh of criticism at the perpetual weariness of older people.
He pulls on his trousers and shirt. Fumbles for his sandals, stuffs his revolver into his trouser pocket and is ready for an exploratory sortie.
The door squeaks; it is also hard to close. But after some patient persuasion there he is, anyway, out in the dizzy expanses of the hotel corridor, flanked by tall white doors and traversed by other corridors vanishing into the distance on either side. Here and there a glimmer of light from some big

113

window, half-hidden behind heavy draperies. In recesses and niches he catches a glimpse of statues, representing a naked lady, or a petrified gentleman.

The boy feels a shiver of anxiety, an elated desire for adventure. Leaving all safety behind he slips away.

The hotel room was stuffy; out here reigns a moldy chill. Johan shivers slightly. Hearing footsteps, he darts in to one side, hides behind a bulging gilt armchair and frees the safety catch of his revolver. A workman in blue overalls with big moustaches and a swollen red face swings into sight round the corner and hurries away. He is carrying a very long ladder. As he breathes, he involuntarily gives out a sharp whistle.

At the end of the corridor he raises his ladder, climbs laboriously up to one of the antiquated lamps. The boy, who has all the time been covering him with his revolver, decides he is harmless, resets the safety catch and slips secretively along his way.

Now he is standing in front of a dark cubbyhole. From the ceiling a sky-light allows a minimum of light to filter down, revealing the floor-waiter. He is sitting in a worn leather armchair with a newspaper on his knee, which, however, he does not read, but just stares unmoving before him, sunk as it were in a wide awake absence of mind. The innumerable lines and wrinkles have deepened immensely, his glasses have slipped down, his eyes seem waxlike, artificial; his mouth, tightly closed, is no more than a thin grey line.

Then a bell rings, a little white indicator tab falls down on the bell-board showing the number; the man instantly gets up and smoothes out his apron. Catching sight of Johan, he says something to him. But the boy doesn't reply, stands there, hesitant, poised for flight. As the old man comes quickly toward him he takes to his heels, swerves round one corner, then another, and so comes to a stop, the pulses in his throat beating madly.

Listens. All quiet again.

A tall narrow window looks out over a blank wall, so near and so tall that only a little grey daylight filters down from above it.

He turns round.

A very small man with a big hooked nose, round eyes and a fringe hurries by. Since this peculiar person is even smaller than himself Johan is not scared, but greets him politely. The man replies to his greeting, then vanishes through a half-open door further on.

On the wall opposite the window a painting hangs in its gilt frame. It represents a fat, entirely naked lady, fighting with a man in hairy fur pants

114

and with hooves in lieu of feet. The lady is very pink, and the dark brown man is covered with hair. On closer inspection the lady, to judge from her stupid smile, doesn't seem altogether displeased by his attentions.

Johan is so busy studying the painting he doesn't notice the waiter approaching. When he does, he realizes it's no good running away.

The old man stops, bends down, puts out his hand; but Johan beats a hasty retreat, energetically shaking his head.

Then the old fellow suddenly gives an agile skip forward, grabs the boy by the arm. For a moment he manages to hold him fast; but Johan wrenches himself free.

The waiter shouts something, but doesn't give chase.

An open door. The very large room within is bathed in sharp sunlight. Beds, tall windows, two huge cupboards with mirrors and carvings, a bulging sofa and three tremendous armchairs.

Along the walls are wooden crates, trunks, half unpacked suitcases, strange objects, scattered everywhere on the floor and furniture.

Five very little people are moving swiftly about, talking and gesticulating, intensely busy.

On the edge of the bed sits a very fat elderly man with grey-white hair and birdlike eyes. He is sewing a little dress. He waves to Johan and says something in his own incomprehensible tongue.

The door closes behind him.

A little old man with a big lion mask on his head jumps forward and growls, pretends to take a bite at Johan's leg; but the boy isn't particularly frightened, draws his revolver and fires. They all laugh and the monster throws itself on the floor as if given its death wound.

Some of the little creatures are wearing pale-colored shiny suits.

A young man is standing at one end of the bed. Clinging to the bedstead, he lifts his legs high up its sides.

Two old men in gaudy coats and with yellowish shiny faces sit slumped in armchairs. They have glasses in their hands, and on the table stand empty bottles.

They look at Johan and laugh.

Johan aims his revolver at them and they pretend to be terrified. One of them crouches down behind the arm of his chair, trembling violently. The other whines and whimpers.

Panting heavily, the fat man on the bed clambers down to the floor and comes waddling up to Johan, holds up his arms and slips the dress over his head.

The boy who had been doing leg exercises begins to laugh, runs up to Johan, takes both his cheeks in his hands, kisses him and begins talking in distraught tones with the old man.

All gather round Johan. He is a little embarrassed by his get up, but not at all frightened. They poke him and pat him on the head, one of them offers a gilded ball. Another begins playing a mouth organ and the third proffers him a peach.

The old man with the lion mask changes into an ape, trying to draw the others' attention by leaping wildly about in every conceivable way.

The door opens and with a self-important air the little man from the corridor steps in.

Immediately all the others are abashed. Their laughter and chatter falls silent. When he sees Johan in the gaudy dress the little man gets angry and orders the fat one to take it off him at once.

He sniffs the air with his big nose and points at one of the old men in the armchairs, giving him a sharp reprimand. In a hang-dog sort of way the latter begins gathering up the beer bottles.

With polite apologies the little man turns to Johan and points to the door.

Johan goes wordlessly out into the corridor. As the door closes behind him, he hears a sharp dark voice speaking within.

Once again he is standing beneath the picture of the pink lady and the fellow in hairy long pants; in the distance he hears the howling of air-raid sirens, only suppressed, in a world remote.

In a new and frightening way the solitude closes in around him and he finds he urgently needs to pee; looks anxiously about him for a toilet. None is to be seen. He runs round a corner to look, again without result.

Quickly he sets off for his own room, but soon realizes he has lost his way among the corridors.

Resigned, he stands and relieves himself in a corner. It turns into quite a river, with many little streams, dividing, all running toward the red carpet.

When he has finished he stuffs his hands into his trouser pockets and whistles.

But it doesn't help much.

He takes a few steps. Actually he is worried to find himself in such a predicament. Looking up from the pattern on the carpet he catches a glimpse of the old waiter at the other end of the corridor.

Johan goes closer.

The waiter beckons. Don't be scared, there's no danger. Takes off his glasses, smiles, baring his big horse-teeth.

116

IV

Anna wakes up out of her deep doze, the sun has moved round and is blazing straight down on the windows, the heat is unstirring, stifling.
She gets out of bed and looks about for Johan, opens the door to Ester's room.

ANNA: Is Johan here?

ESTER: No, he isn't here.

Anna leaves the door open, goes into the bathroom, soaks a towel in cold water and splashes it over her body to cool herself. In the mirror, deep inside the other room, she can see Ester.

Anna looks in her suitcase and gets out some clean underclothes and a light sleeveless summer dress; with quick impatient movements she dresses herself and begins combing her thick hair.

ESTER: How brown you've got.

Anna doesn't reply. Already, tiny spots of gleaming damp are forcing themselves out on her upper lip and forehead; she paints her mouth, meets her own glance in her hazy hand-mirror. Deep down inside her fair eyes one catches a glimpse of wrath and scorn.

She throws the mirror on the table, takes her handbag, gets into her pointed high-heeled shoes.

ANNA: I'm going out a bit.

ESTER: Wait.

ANNA: What's the matter?

She stands leaning against the doorpost, inspecting her nails, biting off a corner of loose skin on her forefinger.

ESTER: Nothing. It's nothing.

Anna goes. She doesn't look back. As the door closes, Ester puts her hand to her mouth as if to stifle a scream.

She fumbles about for some support, turns round, clings to the end of the bed, reaches for the cognac bottle, gets the cork out and forces the neck of the bottle between her chattering teeth. Swallows a few gulps, is convulsed by cramps, drops the bottle, which spills its contents over bedclothes and floor.

She whimpers and swears by turns: it's so humiliating all this, I'm just not going to put up with such humiliation.

Tries to get up off the bed, immediately loses her balance and falls over. Stands on all fours, whimpering like a dog: now I must think clearly. After all, I'm known for my logical, clear head.

117

Stands the bottle upright and rolls up the dusty bedside mat, which has had the worst of it, kneels and picks up the blanket.

Kneels with her hands stretched out across the bed, oh God, help me, let me die at home at least, now I feel a bit better, must try and eat something, my stomach's quite empty, idiotic, drinking on an empty stomach.

She gets up, finds the bell, rings.

After a few moments the old floor waiter is there; picks her up, places her in a chair, pulls out the sheets and bedclothes and flings the whole lot out of the door, takes off the cover from the other bed, helps her round to it, lifts her feet up, arranges the pillows, washes her face and gives her comb and mirror.

Vanishes a moment, but is immediately back with a steamy bottle of mineral water, pours out a glass, which he helps her to drink. She makes a sign to show she wants something to eat, he nods, understands, points to his stomach, an eloquent circular movement, shakes his head. Silently closes the door as he goes.

She leans back against the pillows, somewhere inside her she feels a throbbing desire to vomit.

She closes her eyes and thinks of the Swedish archipelago, a summer outing, the clear green chill of the water, the white horizon, light afternoon clouds over the cliffs.

V

The shadow has moved up the walls of the houses. With a shattering uproar a car with a loudspeaker is gliding along the street; it turns the corner by the church.

Once again the stifling airless silence closes in on the swarming crowds, pulsing along densely packed pavements.

Anna has found her way into the red twilight of the bar. She finds a little table in the crush and points to an iced coffee advertised at the counter.

The man who serves her is very young. A heavy serious face, thick close-cropped hair and clean-shaven cheeks.

He is wearing a soiled white jacket and sweats profusely. Now and then he passes his serviette over his face. His fingers are brown with nicotine and have dark nails. In spite of all the hurry he moves swiftly and calmly.

As he bends down and lights her cigarette, he gives her a friendly smile.

A newspaper vendor appears with a bunch of papers under his arm. She buys one and glances vaguely at the incomprehensible headlines.

118

Notices and advertisements. In large letters: J. S. BACH.
Suddenly the young waiter is back, holds up the coffee pot, she nods assent
and he serves her again. She wants to pay, he writes the figure down on a
little scrap of paper where already there are many others.
She puts down a bank note, and he digs into his pocket, shrugs his shoulders,
grabs up the money and goes up to the counter.
His close-cropped neck is extremely sunburned and his socks in the sandals
have holes in them. Over at the counter he stands on tiptoe, hoisting himself
up as if impatient, waves the note, holding it between thumb and fore-
finger.
He turns round, meets her glance.
Now someone is there, changing her money. Immediately he's back again,
lays the coins on the table, his cigarette lighter falls to the floor, swiftly
he bends down. For a brief moment his chin brushes against her
thigh.
Then he is gone, bending politely over another of the pavement tables, hold-
ing his little pad high before him.
Indifferent, she follows him with her glance, stifling a yawn. The cigarette
smoke lies heavy and dense; on the ceiling the fans spin in vain.
She makes her way among the tables, feeling this silence like a lid over her
ears; silence as a dull, thumping fear.

VI

Ester has been given a tray of food. She is eating cautiously, swallowing
little gulps of water, and resting between whiles. Johan is standing in the
doorway. He still has his hands in his trouser pockets, but looks rather
miserable.

ESTER: Are you hungry?

JOHAN (*nods*).

ESTER: Come and have some of my food.

She takes the lid off a vegetable dish and he sits on the edge of her bed and
eats hungrily.

ESTER: Longing to get home?

JOHAN (*nods seriously*).

ESTER: On Monday we'll be there.

JOHAN: Can I go to Granny then?

ESTER: Yes, straight away.

JOHAN: How long for?

ESTER: First the whole summer, then the winter. You're going to go to school at Granny's.

JOHAN: D'you think Mom'll come and see me?

ESTER: Of course.

JOHAN: Is it nice with Granny in the country?

ESTER: It's lovely. You'll live in a big house with lots of rooms and the sun shines almost all the time.

JOHAN: Will Daddy come too?

ESTER: I think so. If he has time. But he's always so busy.

JOHAN: Yes, he is.

ESTER: But there's lots of other lovely things to do there. A whole lot of horses . . .

JOHAN: I'm scared of horses.

ESTER: And rabbits. And you can go sailing with Uncle Persson. The water's quite clear and green. You can see the bottom, even though it's terribly deep. (*Pause*) You mustn't be sad.

JOHAN (*quietly*): I'm not sad.

ESTER: And in the autumn you can catch crayfish.

JOHAN: Will *you* come and see me?

ESTER: You can go down to the old jetty. And fish! What d'you like fishing for most? You like to go fishing, don't you?

JOHAN: Perch. But we get roach, too.

The conversation dies away. They fall silent. Ester puts out her hand and touches Johan's cheek and ear, mostly as a caress. He shies away with an expression of surprise but since his mouth is full of food doesn't say anything.

ESTER: You can go back to your own room if you've had enough.

JOHAN: Thanks for the food. I'm really full.

He keeps a polite distance; jumps down off the bed, goes toward the other room.

ESTER: Leave the door open, there's a good boy.

JOHAN: I'll make you a lovely painting if you like.

Ester nods. Tenderness for the boy, and fear. All these confused thoughts.

JOHAN: You mustn't worry. Mom'll soon be back. Besides, I'm here.

Ester turns her gaze toward the window.

Without waiting for an answer he withdraws into the other room, where he searches about until he finds his crayons and drawing pad. Then he makes a long red line, which continues in a bow and forms itself into a forehead, a nose, a cruel twisted mouth.

120

VII

At the pavement café Anna stands indecisive among the midday crowds.
The sun thunders down over walls, roofs and windowpanes.
To shelter from the heat, but also so as not to have to go home (the entrance
of the hotel is just across the street) she takes refuge again in the gloom of
the bar.
To the left of the counter is a short stairway and an open door leading
into the neighboring movie theater.
Large notices announce the program and out of the narrow foyer a
pleasing coolness streams towards her.
She buys a ticket and is shown in through a door in the curving wall.
An elderly usher lights her way with his pocket flashlight and in the
darkness she glimpses a reddish-colored seat. She is in a box, separated
from the orchestra by a high barrier.
By and by, on the other side of the narrow aisle, she makes out the dim
forms of a man and a woman. They are sitting leaning against each other
in a tight embrace and pay no heed to her arrival.
She can make no sense of the film being shown, it seems incomprehensible.
A comedian wholly devoid of comedy, but heavily made up and fantastic-
ally decked out, is playing a ruined piano.
Beside him but facing the other way sits a woman with a swelling
curvaceous figure. She has a mirror in front of her and is fixing her
make-up.
All the time as she does so she speaks in wrathful accents, interrupted from
time to time by deep sighs. The clown pays no attention whatever to the
woman. Not even when she turns round and places her anatomy on the
keyboard and her mirror upon the piano does he bother about her.
Just goes on squeezing strange agonizing sequences of notes out of his
instrument. As she starts powdering herself in a cloud of powder from a
big powderpuff the clown vanishes.
The cloud disperses and he is sitting alone on a big dark stage with a
double bass. He begins playing on it with a thick, rounded bow.
Anna, yawning, has been watching these strange antics. She lights a
cigarette. Suddenly her interest is caught by the man and the woman. She
can see them better now, her eyes have got used to the darkness.
The man is tall and thin, with sparse, parted hair and heavy eyebrows
that stick out over his eyes, shadowing their expression. The woman is
rather small and has a round white face with large pouting lips and dyed

hair which falls in careless tufts about her ears and down on to her sloping shoulders.

The man is kneeling on the floor and has lifted up her blouse over her chubby little breasts, she is grasping his big ears, pressing his face into her stomach.

Then she leans forward and reaches down her short stubby arms toward the man's lap and begins undoing his zipper, gasping all the while as with a great effort.

Her peroxided hair falls forward over both their faces. With a violent movement the man gets up, throws his arms round the woman who becomes completely motionless, lifts her up from the seat, sits down leaning heavily backward, she fumbles for the edge of her skirt and pulls it up to her stomach, her thick thighs gleam in the darkness.

She leans sharply back toward the barrier, while her hands fumble for support against his knees. His face is turned up, his head thrown back, his throat extended and the big adam's apple raises itself in a lump, as if it was about to burst through the thin envelope of skin.

The reflected light from the screen plays over their fumbling jerky movements.

Anna, hugging the wall, her hand poised with her cigarette, stares absorbedly at this strange scene. The spiral of cigarette smoke goes upward through the light toward the darkness under the ceiling.

In the loudspeakers the clown's jibberish goes on and on, interrupted occasionally by a few growling notes or chords.

Anna gets up, drops her cigarette, fumbles for the door and is immediately out in the dirty cramped foyer, with its bright-coloured posters and gaudy photos of unknown stars.

Dizzy, weighed down by her body, exhausted, she supports herself against the wall. Someone throws her an indifferent glance. Slowly she goes out into the stifling grey afternoon light.

Confused and at a loose end, she follows the stream of pedestrians down toward the bar.

In front of the barriers round the pavement tables she stops and looks about, searching for someone.

The waiter is standing among the tables, involved in a discussion with an older colleague. At first he doesn't seem to notice her, but then, still talking, he turns his head and observes her.

She looks quickly away.

VIII

Johan is spying on the old waiter, who has again sat down in his cubby-hole.

He has laid out his dinner before him: a bottle of beer and some sandwiches in a tin box, also a tiny bottle with a screw-top, which also serves as a beaker, and which he balances adroitly.

Holding the brimming cap between thumb and forefinger, he opens his mouth, throws his head back and with a swift movement tips the drink in between his long teeth.

Several times he repeats this maneuvre.

Catching sight of Johan, the waiter bursts out laughing. Johan doesn't like being laughed at, gets a bit angry, and is on the verge of going. At once the waiter stops laughing, calls him back.

The boy turns round. The old man has fished out a bar of chocolate from his lunch case and is waving it in the air. The temptation is too great.

Johan goes up to the old man, shakes hands, bows, a little deep nod (as becomes a Swedish boy who wants to be polite), and is made a present of half the bar of chocolate, sits down on a turned-up crate and munches it. With a strange scraping noise, the old man chews his food, now and again sucking his teeth. This makes Johan, in his turn, burst out laughing.

The waiter looks at him. Mostly for company's sake he laughs, too. Begins searching in his big black wallet and brings out some photos. They show a country house behind a big tree, an old woman in an open coffin, surrounded by friends and relations, also some pictures of children of various ages and variously dressed.

Between mouthfuls the old man comments on each of these pictures, though for the most part only with little convulsive sighs. Takes off his glasses and wipes them. At the base of his nose a tear has fastened. He squashes it with his forefinger, makes an expressive gesture which can mean: all dead and gone, finished.

This motivates another turn of the screw-cap and a generous swig of beer, the crinkled cheeks come out in red patches, the shaded eyes become wet. His hands with their liver-colored spots clasped tightly, he sinks into deep ponderings, now and then muttering to himself. Suddenly, he lays his arm round Johan's shoulders and draws him to him.

The boy isn't frightened, doesn't resist; just sits there quietly, letting the old man pat him on the shoulder.

For quite a long while they sit together like this.

Hearing his mother's footsteps in the corridor Johan gently disengages himself from the old man's arm and makes off round the corner.

He calls after her. She stops and turns round. With outflung arms he rushes toward her, embraces her passionately.

Seizing her right hand in both his own, he half-runs, half-skips along beside her.

When they get to the door she gives him a quick kiss on the top of his head and whispers something in his ear. He nods, understanding.

In a rather melancholy way he hops about on one leg.

Undecided, Anna stands there a few moments and an anxious expression comes over her face. Then she opens the door and goes in. Johan, left alone, goes on hopping, though now on the other leg.

Anna goes straight into the bathroom, turns on the tap in the basin, takes off her pants and lays them in the water. Then she takes off her dress and puts on her dressing gown.

Ester is standing behind her in the doorway. She has put on a white skirt and a thin square-necked silk blouse with short sleeves.

Except for the heavy mascara on her eyelashes her face has no make-up. Round her right wrist she is wearing a heavy silver bracelet. Her hair is gathered up by a strong silver comb.

Anna looks up from what she is doing, notices the wrath in Ester's eyes. At first she is frightened, but instantly controls herself.

ANNA: Feeling better? Well, that's good.

Ester grabs up Anna's dress, which is hanging over the edge of the bath, and holding it up between thumb and forefinger studies it searchingly. Anna doesn't respond, combs her hair out so fiercely that it crackles, searches in her bag for her hairclips, finds them and begins doing her hair. Ester drops the dress on the floor.

Anna gives a scornful snort. Ester's hand, holding a cigarette, begins to tremble. Speechless, beside herself with rage, she leaves her sister.

Anna completes her hair-do and searches in her big carelessly packed suitcase for a pair of clean pants, which she puts on, then makes a few indecisive movements in various directions; toward the door to the corridor, toward a packet of cigarettes on the bedside table, to the wardrobe mirror.

But cruelty rises within her, goes to her head; she enters the next room.

Ester is sitting at the writing desk with her dictionaries, her galley-proofs, and her heaps of notes on loose sheets of paper.

Anna leans both hands on the table. Ester does not look up from her work.

ANNA: What are you up to?

124

ESTER: Working, as you see.

ANNA: Then I think you should stick to your work.

ESTER (*questioning*).

ANNA: And not spy on me.

ESTER: Maybe.

Anna stands leaning over the table, the upper part of her body rocks slightly. Her voice is still completely calm.

ANNA: If only I could understand why I've been so scared.

ESTER: Scared?

ANNA: Scared of you.

She sinks her head deeply, affirmatively, then straightens her back, gathers her housecoat about her.

Seeing Ester's look she gives an enigmatic smile, leaves the room, silently and softly closes the door. At once Ester stops work, stares out of the window at the sun burned wall of the house opposite. A mortal fear of death sweeps over her, from between her clenched white teeth escapes a faint moan.

IX

Johan is standing in the dusky corridor, looking at a creature of immense age. He has never seen such an aged person. The face is quite yellow, the brow high with a wreath of wispy hair round its cranium. Behind the gold spectacles the eyes are childishly blue, staring. Beneath the long thin nose move blueish withered lips. The whole head seems to stand on a very high starched collar, which sticks up out of a tidy but altogether too capacious dark suit.

Fumbling with an elegant cane, panting for breath, the old man moves slowly forward over the soft carpet.

As the sun strikes in through a side corridor, the creature comes to a halt, turning his face toward the sun and Johan.

X

As twilight falls the town's uneasy silence deepens. The narrow street in front of the hotel pulsates with a dark stream of people.

The shop windows slam their heavy iron shutters and the neon lights blink gaudily.

The bells of the brick church fill the air with their roaring and a few children rush shrieking over the steps in front of its gates.

Ester, hyperconscious of everything, is standing at the window, looking and listening. In the shadow of annihilation her awareness quivers.
On the bed in the other room Anna is sitting clipping her son's nails. He enjoys her attentions, though he loathes having his nails manicured.

JOHAN: When are we going home?

ANNA: This evening, maybe.

JOHAN: Is Ester coming too?

ANNA: I don't know.

JOHAN: You're dreadfully angry with her, aren't you?

Anna lifts the lamp on the bedside table, reviews the results of her nail-clipping. Johan lifts his arm and puts it fondly round his mother's neck. She draws him to her and kisses him over and over again; sits a long while silent, rocking him on her knee, in her arms.

JOHAN: What's this town called, Mommy?

ANNA: Tiimoka, I think.

The boy absorbs the name and contemplates it. Whispers it to himself, as he likes to with queer words.
Ester goes into the depths of the room, switches on the little transistor radio they have brought in their baggage. Through the dreamy twilight comes music by Bach. A faint knock at the door. The floor waiter enters. Politely, half-bowed, he asks a question. She shakes her head, no she didn't ring. He apologizes, but remains, listening.

ESTER (*in a low voice*): What's it called. MUSIC?

WAITER (*smiles*): Music—musike! Music—musike.

ESTER: Sebastian Bach?

WAITER (*pleased*): Sebastian Bach. (*Nods emphatically*) Johann Sebastian Bach.

A long while he stands and listens. Comes to. Have a lot to do; bows apologetically, is gone.
Ester sits on a chair by the wall, leaning forward with her arms crossed on her knees; she has kicked off her shoes; her face is bowed down, inwards, she can see her little pulse on the inside of her wrist, just above the black strap of her wrist watch.
The door to the next room opens imperceptibly and Johan is standing there, listening but dubious. Anna is still sitting on her bed, as before, with her profile dark against the light of the bedside lamp.
All three, listening.

ANNA (*in a low voice*): Johan was going to ask you for some cigarettes. Mine are finished.

ESTER: On the desk.

ANNA: Can I take a few?

ESTER: Of course.

ANNA: Thanks. Nice of you.

Obediently Johan fetches a few cigarettes from the writing desk, gives them to his mother. Then goes back to the doorway and sits down on its raised threshold, cupping his chin in his hand.

ESTER: I think you should go on this evening. There's a train in a few hours.

ANNA: What about you?

ESTER: I'll stay.

ANNA: We can't leave you like this.

ESTER: It's better. You need to get home. I'm not strong enough to travel now, anyway. Maybe in a couple of days.

They become still. The music wanders through the dusk. Johan heaves a deep sigh.

ANNA: What music's that?

ESTER: Bach. Sebastian Bach.

Anna gets up and walks to and fro across the floor, impatient but controlled. Ester follows her with her glance. At last she can't control herself any longer, reaches out to the radio and switches it off.

A hostile silence.

Anna looks about her for her bag and gloves.

ANNA: I'm going out a little.

No reply.

ANNA *(more frightened)*: It's so hot, too. You know I can't stand. . . .

No reply. Anna goes over to the doorway, lays her hand on the door knob. Johan looks up at her, questioning.

ANNA: I'll be back soon.

Johan nods, but looks sad.

ANNA: And you'll get a nice big reward if you keep Ester company. You can read aloud to her.

ESTER: Go now, before your bad conscience makes you scream. *(Pause)* Go now.

Anna throws her bag on to a chair, goes into the room and sits down on the bed opposite Ester, passing her fingers over her chin and throat.

ANNA: D'you think you matter in the least? I mean, what you do or say?

Ester contemplates her legs, shrugs her shoulders.

ANNA: Whoever put that notion into your head? That it's up to you to decide?

127

ESTER (*coldly*):   You can't manage on your own.

ANNA: You think you can make my decisions for me, just like Father did. But you can't.

ESTER (*silent*).

ANNA: You think I'm stupid, eh?

ESTER (*smiles*):   I don't think you're stupid.

Ester leans far back in her uncomfortable chair. Stretching her arms up behind her head she touches the wall with her finger. Anna turns to her son. Her voice has changed.

ANNA: Can't you go into the other room awhile and shut the door. I want to talk to Ester. Alone.

Johan, deeply alarmed, gets up, stands hesitant.

JOHAN: Wasn't I to read aloud to Ester?

ANNA: Yes, soon.

JOHAN: I'll go out into the corridor awhile.

ANNA: All right, but don't go too far.

Johan's face is bitter as he looks at his mother. No, he won't go too far. He'll be on hand, in case it pleases her to call for him. But just now she wants no part of him. He's to vanish, instantly.
And does.

The two women are left alone in a dusk that is rapidly turning to darkness. The light from the street aims thick shadows at ceiling and walls. The room becomes an aquarium.

Ester has poured herself out a cognac. She takes cautious sips.

ESTER: Where've you been all the afternoon?

ANNA: Taking a walk in the town.

ESTER: Where did you walk?

ANNA: Just nearby.

ESTER: That was a long walk.

ANNA: I didn't feel like coming back to the hotel.

ESTER: And why not?

ANNA: Just didn't feel like it.

ESTER: You're lying.

ANNA: As if that mattered.

ESTER: What've you been up to?

ANNA: If you don't know, you're stupid.

Ester falls silent a few moments, smokes her cigarette, looks out of the window, the scorn of her smile does not diminish.

ESTER: Where did you find that man?

ANNA: In the bar, just across the street.

128

Anna looks at her sister with a smile.

ANNA: Want to know the details?

ESTER: Answer my questions.

ANNA: D'you remember the winter ten years ago, when we were staying with Father at Lyon? And I'd been with Claude? Remember cross-examining me just the same way? How you scratched my arm and swore you'd tell Father if I didn't tell you all the details?

ESTER *(distressed).*

ANNA: I went into a movie theater and sat in a box at the back of the orchestra. There was a man and a woman who began making love. Under my very nose. When they'd finished they went out. After a while the boy from the bar came in and sat down beside me and began stroking my thighs. Then we lay on the floor. That's how my dress got dirty.

ESTER: Is that all true?

ANNA: Why should I tell lies?

ESTER *(dully)*: Yes, why should you tell lies?

ANNA: Though as it happens, I am.

ESTER: It doesn't matter.

Ester has crumpled into grey exhaustion, a tormented grimace.

ANNA: I looked at that couple who were making love. Then I went out, down to the bar, and the boy followed me, but we didn't really know where to go, so we went into the church and made love in a dark corner behind a pair of big pillars.—At least it wasn't so hot there.

ESTER *(after a pause)*: Are you meeting him again?

ANNA: I was just on my way when you began talking. He's waiting for me.

ESTER. I understand.

ANNA: This time I'll make sure I've time to take my clothes off.

Averted, with hunched shoulders, Ester stands by the desk lamp, lights it, switches it off.

ESTER: Why've we got to torment each other?

ANNA: You aren't tormenting me.

Ester turns and Anna sees her sister's swollen flaming face, the hazy dark eyes, the open trembling mouth.

ANNA: Shouldn't you lie down?

ESTER *(tired)*: Yes.

129

Collapsed on the bed, she clings to Anna with her strong thin arms, presses her feverish mouth against her sister's neck. Anna frees herself.

ESTER: Sit with me here on the edge of the bed.

ANNA *(shakes her head)*.

ESTER: One little moment.

Anna picks up her bag and sits down at the far end, at the foot of the bed, waiting to see what will happen.

ANNA: Well?

ESTER: Are you going to meet him?

ANNA *(nods)*.

ESTER: Can't you give it up? Just now, just this evening.

ANNA *(silent)*.

ESTER: It torments me.

ANNA: Does it? Why?

ESTER: Because . . . Because I feel so humiliated. Don't think I'm jealous.

The last in a whisper, with wide-staring eyes, her hand fumbling for Anna's.

ANNA: I'll go now.

XI

He is waiting for her in the corridor, seizes her arms, kisses her, she presses herself to him. In the sleepy light from the yellow electric lamps in their antique iron holders they do not see Johan, standing a couple of yards further off.

The man goes behind her with one hand on her shoulder. They stop in front of a door, he feels in his pocket, brings out a key, unlocks it.

Johan sees the door close behind them.

He sits down in a gilded armchair, leaning forward, chewing his lower lip, swallowing his grief and fury.

The room is narrow but with a high ceiling, the shutters are closed, in the greyish fleeting light furniture and objects can be faintly seen. The heat is stifling. A smell of dust and old woodwork. A cupboard with a long mirror leans out from the wall. The bed's pillow and bolster gleam faintly.

Silent, without touching each other, they undress.

Johan stands outside the door, listening. He hears his mother's voice, softly whimpering, the rustle of bedclothes, the man's whisperings.

She laughs, but her laugh is strange and ends in a stifled cry. Johan takes

130

*a few steps backwards. Then he runs away, into his own and his mother's
room.*

*Ester's door is closed, the light burns on the bedside table. Around him all
is still.*

*He takes a book out of the open suitcase, lays it on the bed, turns its pages
idly, looks at the simple colored pictures.*

*Shuts the book and pads in to Ester who has dropped off to sleep on her
bed. Her mouth is open. She snores faintly.*

Her face has sunk in, seems strange. One hand moves, its fingers twitch.

*Johan goes over to the window, which is ajar, and looks down into the street,
all empty now and silent.*

*Lights advertising the bar and the movie. Blue trembling street-lights.
Heat against the house walls.*

Scared by the dull, anxious stillness, he withdraws his head.

*On the writing desk lie a few pieces of paper, scribbled all over in Ester's
microscopic handwriting.*

*One or two, however, are written in large printed capitals. There is
HADJEK = spirit, MAGROV = anxiety, fear, KRASGT = joy. After
these she had written: "We listened to BACH. A moment of peace. I felt no
fear of dying."*

*Johan puts out the desk lamp and stands listening in the dark. Through
the soles of his feet he can feel the floor quivering slightly. He hears a faint
tinkling, notices that a drinking glass is rattling against its carafe.
Through the silence a rattling rumbling murmur rises and falls, as of a
heavy machine at work. He clambers up into the window and looks each
way down the street. At first it is as empty and deserted as before.*

*But after a few moments a shapeless shadow frees itself out of the dusk by
the church steps. Takes shape, swings with a heavy crashing noise down the
narrow street and rolls slowly down towards the next side street.*

*It stops, all sounds cease, the glass no longer trembles against the side of its
carafe, the floor no longer quivers beneath Johan's foot. The tank stands
motionless. Expectant. Threatening. No sign of anyone.*

*Johan turns his glance to Ester, sees she's awake and is observing him with
a strange wide-eyed gaze.*

ESTER (*gently*):   You were going to read to me.

*Johan hangs his head. An inexpressible anxiety, Ester's strange look, her
strange hoarse voice, all make him feel drowsy.*

JOHAN: How funny you look.

*Ester smiles, but the smile fastens between her teeth and she draws a deep
breath.*

ESTER: Will you read to me now?

JOHAN: I'll put on a play for you instead.

He runs into the other room and in the suitcase finds a brown cardboard box. In the box he has his puppets—a few splendid glove-puppets of cloth. He brings out Mr. Punch and the little old woman, thrust his hands inside them and hides behind the end of the bed, making the puppets jump up over the edge.

PUNCH (*raging, furious*): Utji utji brrr kollepastimos fritrabuntil karhpestapista alla bom! Alla bom alla bom urr stakrafast.

LITTLE OLD WOMAN (*frightened*): Dear Mr. Punch, oh, oh, Punch dear oh, piss piss piss.

PUNCH (*beside himself, hitting her furiously*): Hoffra kollipenna mossbill kurradown rarasipäl hoy hoy!

The puppets fight, the old woman screams and weeps. Punch rages.

In the end the little old woman dies, or at least disappears behind the end of the bed.

JOHAN: Now he doesn't know what to do, because the old woman is dead.

PUNCH (*livid*): Ulipiss pissipisspiss!

ESTER: What's he saying?

JOHAN: How should I know? He's talking in a funny language. Because he's frightened.

ESTER: Can't Punch sing something today?

JOHAN: Sure. But not until he's not so angry.

Punch leaps up and down. Vanishes behind the end of the bed.

Silence.

Instead Johan, red in the face, rushes out, crying. He creeps up to Ester in the bed, she throws her arms round him, over his head and cheeks, feels his breath, his thumping heart.

So they lie still together, listening to the rattling roar of the tank's motor. It swings round the corner, is gone.

Anna has got out of bed and opened the window shutters, stands looking down into a narrow well.

Far beneath there is a square of light, a large skylight, with a net across it, guarded by iron bars.

Beneath the dirty, half-illuminated square of light a glimpse of people moving to and fro, busily rushing hither and thither like ants.

But not a sound, not a single sound forces its way up from the well. She leans out, the weak light from the night sky falling over her shoulders and the untidy mass of her hair.

132

The man sits hunched in the bed, with his chin resting on his knees and his back against the wall.
Closely she studies his face, his mouth, his eyes. They can make each other out quite clearly in the half-light.
She takes his hand, looks at his black broken fingernails, touches a broad scar on his arm.
She presses it with her nail, he reacts with a smile, uninterested, but his gaze is turned toward the lighter rectangle of the window.

ANNA: How nice you are. How nice it is we don't understand each other.

Her hand caresses his hip, his stomach, feels between his legs.

ANNA: I wish Ester was dead.

She brings her face close to his. He nods affirmatively, and lays his head on her breast.

XII

Johan is about to go to bed for the night. Brushes his teeth. Gargles, spits, washes out the handbasin.
Gets into his mother's bed with a book and an apple, glasses on his nose.
Through the open door between the rooms he can see Ester in a thick cloud of cigarette smoke sitting at her writing desk.

JOHAN: Why are you a translator?

ESTER: If a book's written in a foreign language, I translate it so you can read it.

JOHAN: Do you know the language in this country?

ESTER: No, but I've learned a few words.

Johan thinks this over, takes some bites at his apple, becomes very serious.

JOHAN: You mustn't forget to write those words down for me.

ESTER: I shan't forget.

JOHAN: Ester.

ESTER: Yes.

JOHAN: Why doesn't Mommy want to be with us?

ESTER: But she does.

JOHAN: No. She beats it at the first opportunity.

ESTER: She's just gone for a walk.

JOHAN: No, she hasn't.

ESTER (*silent*).

133

JOHAN: She's with someone in a room. They were kissing like mad and then they beat it into a room off the corridor. I saw it myself.

ESTER: Are you sure?

JOHAN: Well, I saw it, didn't I?

Ester is standing in the doorway, looking at the boy. He is sitting in the middle of the swelling softness of the bed, trying to read; but his face is contracted with pain.

She goes over to him, touches his downy hair and his frail long neck, allows her fingers to glide over his big soft ears.

ESTER: Have you washed properly?

JOHAN (*sadly*): No. Must I?

ESTER: And we thought our trip would be such fun. A lovely pleasure trip to the most beautiful place on earth. And it turned into . . .

JOHAN (*politely*): I've had a lot of fun.

She caresses the boy's head and cheek; he finds it too much to bear, makes a little movement to one side.

She withdraws her hand.

ESTER: It's only Mommy, I suppose, who's allowed to touch you?

JOHAN (*remains silent, faintly embarrassed*).

ESTER: We love Mommy, you and I.

She smiles. Johan stares at his book, without reading. On the right is a fine picture of Robin Hood in the green forest. He is stretching his bow, aiming at a deer.

ESTER: D'you know what they say for 'face' in this country's language? (*Pause*) It's called NAJGO, and hand is KASI.

JOHAN (*nods*): Oh?

Ester lightly touches his shoulder.

ESTER: Night night.

JOHAN: Night night.

ESTER: Mind if I shut the door?

JOHAN: 'Course not. I don't mind.

ESTER: Mommy'll be here soon.

JOHAN (*doesn't reply*).

XIII

Anna has begun to get dressed again, but is sitting with her dress in her hand. The man has lit the hard little light above the washstand and is elaborately combing his hair.

ANNA: When she's ill. She's always ill. When she's ill, she wants to decide everything. Then I'm a half-wit.

She passes her hand over her knee, pouts, cocks her head.

ANNA: "You're a greedy pig", she says. "How fat you've got these last months. You'll have to slim." I like food (*Yawns*). So would she, if only she didn't drink so much.

Anna places herself behind the man, looks at him in the mirror. Serious, he meets her gaze.

Someone is at the door, the handle is being cautiously thrust down. A knock.

The handle jumps up with a little thump.

Anna listens. Reaches over and switches out the light; at first the room becomes impenetrably dark, but by and by two shadows can be dimly discerned against the window's grey patch of nocturnal light.

In the silence can be heard Ester's heavy breathing, the flat of her hand being placed against the wall, her suppressed but irrepressible weeping.

ANNA: She's still there. (*Pause*) She's crying.

Anna embraces the man and kisses him, takes him by the hand and leads him toward the bed. On bare feet she glides back to the door, turns the key, opens, runs to the bed, snuggles down, draws the man to her.

Ester, confused in the stifling darkness, hears movements from the bed, approaches, feeling her way.

The lamp on the bedside table tinkles against the marble slab. The sudden light is red and murky, reflected whitely on the ceiling.

Anna lays her arm round the man's neck and pretends to make herself comfortable, but he moves away from her, up against the wall.

Ester has gone over to the window, looks out into the yard below and the little square of night sky, grey and dirty from the town's lights.

ESTER: Why've you got to revenge yourself all the time?

ANNA (*silent*).

A long silence.

ESTER: When Father was alive . . .

ANNA: When Father was alive he decided things. And we obeyed him. Because we had to. When Father died you thought you could carry on in the same way. And went on about your principles, how meaningful everything was, how important! But it was just a lot of poppycock. (*Pause*) D'you know why? I'll tell you why. It was all in aid of your self-importance. You can't live without your sense of your own importance. And that's the truth of it. You can't *bear* it if everything isn't "a matter of life and death" and "significant" and "meaningful" and I don't know what else.

Cautiously, Ester sits down, lays her arms on the table. Every movement she makes is careful, as if the least violence could cause her physical pain.

ESTER (*calmly*): How do you want us to live, then? After all, we own everything in common.

ANNA (*calmer*): I always thought you were right. And tried to be like you. And I admired you. I didn't realize you disliked me.

ESTER: It's not true.

ANNA: You dislike me. And always have. Though it's only now I've realized it.

ESTER: No.

ANNA: Yes! In some way I can't understand, you're scared of me.

ESTER: I'm not scared, Anna. I love you.

ANNA (*scorn*): You're always talking about love.

Ester is about to reply, but just gapes. After a few moments' silence her lips begin to move, but her voice isn't equal to it and all she utters is an unclear whisper.

ESTER: You mustn't say . . .

ANNA (*coldly*): What mustn't I say? That Ester hates. That's just a silly invention of silly Anna. You hate me, just like you hate yourself. And me. And everything that's mine. *You're full of hate.*

ESTER: You've got it all wrong.

ANNA: You who're so intelligent, who've taken so many exams and translated so many books, can you answer me just one thing? (*Pause*) When Father died you said: "Now I don't want to live any longer." Well, why do you live, then?

ESTER (*doesn't reply*).

ANNA: For my sake? For Johan? (*Pause*) For your work, perhaps? (*Pause*) Or for nothing in particular?

A long silence.

136

ESTER: It's not as you say. I'm *sure* you're wrong.
ANNA (*screams*):   Stop it! Drop that tone of voice!
ESTER (*doesn't reply*).
ANNA (*screams*):   Go away! Get out! Let me alone!
Ester has been sitting looking down. Now she raises her head and contemplates her sister.
ESTER: Poor Anna.
ANNA: Can't you be quiet!
Ester gets up, goes to the door. Her face is completely calm. Its petrified expression of pain has dissolved and been succeeded by an almost imperceptible smile.
She looks at her sister, without superiority, sympathetically, with tenderness. Slowly she closes the door behind her.
Anna, wildly laughing, throws herself against the wall. When the man touches her shoulder she hits him across the mouth.
Her laughter turns into heavy weeping, she throws herself on one side against the head of the bed, her head tosses to and fro and the thick hair straggles across her arm.
He leans over her, begins to mumble to her imploringly, kisses her neck, her back, lays his hands on her thighs.
She gives the frail bedside table a kick, the lamp falls to the floor, burns furiously an instant and with a faint sharp tinkling sound goes out.
She lies prone over the end of the bed tightly holding its iron posts, raises her face upwards; for a moment she sees a glimpse of the dirty grey square of light above the yard.
Dawn is coloring it a pale yellow.
Ester has supported herself against the wall out in the corridor, which is bathed in a dim nocturnal light.
Out of the silence arises the sound of many chattering voices.
The noise comes nearer, and a caravan of wildly excited, splendidly apparelled dwarfs comes marching round the corner toward her in the corridor.
Theatrically made up in exaggerated masks, they are wearing shapeless costumes, big pointed hats.
Many are inebriated, stagger, hold each other up, laughing.
Someone begins to sing, skips a few steps of a dance, the others hush and giggle. They notice Ester, fall silent, salute her with exaggerated mocking politeness.
After they have passed, the last one in the procession runs back a few steps and asks her something.

137

Getting no answer, he rejoins the others.
Round the corner, they burst out into resounding laughter.
Ester makes a few movements with her arms, presses her shoulders to-
gether, opens her mouth. A thin stream of blood runs quietly down over her
chin, flecks her skirt and drips onto the carpet.
She stands still, with surprised, wide-awake eyes, trying to draw breath.

XIV

It has grown lighter over the yard and from the church can be heard the
tolling of a bell summoning people to early communion.
Anna drinks thirstily the water which squirts out of the hand-basin tap,
straightens out her hair, looks at herself in the mirror. A grey morning
light fills the room.
Sharp contours and a thin stream of cool air.
The man is lying on his face in the bed, sunken in a deep coma, one arm
hangs over the edge, its fingers touching the floor, a black growth of beard
has grown on his chin and cheeks.
Anna, without waking him, soundlessly presses down the door handle and
tries to open it. Someone is resisting, and the handle only yields slowly.
She presses it down with all her force.
Now there is a glimpse of a shoulder, a head, a leg sprawled out over the
carpet. She lets go of the door, crouches on the floor, reaches out her arms
toward the head.

XV

The noon heat leans heavily against the walls of houses and pours in
through the open window.
News vendors' cries. The dull movement of the human mass crowded on
narrow pavements. A few shrieking rhythms from a loudspeaker.
Ester is half sitting up in bed with three pillows at her back.
The old floor waiter sits hunched on a chair at the foot of the bed. Now
and then he gets up to give her some lemon juice from a steamy carafe on
the bedside table.
Anna has just finished packing. Johan is sitting on the floor with
his book.
ANNA: Johan and I'll just slip across the road for a bite to eat.
ESTER (*nods without answering*).

138

ANNA: Then I'll pay Johan's and my bill.

ESTER (*closes her eyes*).

ANNA: We're taking a train which leaves at two.

ESTER (*nods*).

ANNA: A doctor's coming as soon as possible. I don't know, I don't understand a word—but it seemed as if . . .

ESTER: Thank you.

ANNA (*distressed*): It's dreadfully hot.

Tiny pearls of sweat shine on her cheeks and on her upper lip.

ESTER: What's that perfume you've got on?

ANNA: The one you gave me.

ESTER: You shouldn't put so much on in this heat.

Anna goes into the next room, says something to Johan, who at once shuts his book. He is dressed for the journey and pulls up his half-length socks.

JOHAN: Bye, then. I'll soon be back.

ESTER: Bye bye.

Anna and Johan converse quietly by the window, then go out into the corridor and lock the door to their room.

Ester is alone with the old waiter.

She reaches for the glass; immediately he is there, supporting her and helping her to drink. She thanks him and asks for her notes which are lying on the writing table. To support them he gives her the writing pad, puts the fountain pen in her hand. Immediately she begins writing in capitals: "To JOHAN, a few words of the foreign language." Still in capitals, she writes down a row of words.

The effort exhausts her. She rests her head on the pillows piled up behind her back, closes her eyes, listens.

Down in the street she hears a child crying. The piercing wavering note arises out of the dull stream of muted noises.

If she turns her head she can hear the fast hard ticking of a clock.

She opens her eyes: the old waiter, sunk in an armchair, has taken out his big gold watch and is studying it reflectively; with a little watch key which hangs from his watchchain, he begins winding it up.

The child's crying ceases. The curtain bellies in a gust of air.

Slowly consciousness drains away. Her face becomes grey and swollen; her eyes grow wider, her voice irritable and shrill.

ESTER: She's been gone an hour. And with the boy, too.

She laughs bitterly, strikes the bolster with the flat of her hand; her fountain pen rolls down on to the floor. The waiter gets up, recovers it, lays it on the bedside table.

ESTER: It's because the blood-vessels are overflowing, and all
the mucous. Before supreme unction, a confession. I think
semen smells nasty. You see, I've a sensitive nose. I found I
stank like a rotten fish after being fructified. Ah well, it's
optional.

*With the sheet she dries herself under the left armpit and slips down in
bed, exposing one leg. Paper, writing-pad, pillows all fall to the floor.
Once again the waiter rises, begins to gather them up. She reaches out a
hand, lays it on his head.*

ESTER: It's a silly part, and I don't want to play it. Still, it's
nice to be alone now.

*Head bowed, the old man kneels with the writing pad in his hand, his
cranium close to her big dry mouth. He does not stir.*

ESTER: We try them out, one attitude after another, and find them
all meaningless. The powers are too strong for us, I mean
the *monstrous* powers. You have to take care, moving among
ghosts and memories. (*Laughs*) Let me tell you!

*She takes her hand away from the old man's head, looks up at the ceiling's
heavy plaster ornaments.*

ESTER (*quietly*): I'm babbling. (*Still more quiet*) Anyway it's
something to die.

A long moment of silence.

*The old man is standing at the foot of the bed. His hands rest on the back
of a chair, his watch ticks in his vest pocket, somewhere, far off, a
piano can be heard playing but only intermittent notes reach her consciousness.*

ESTER: No need to start a discussion about loneliness. That's
quite superfluous. Give me my writing things.

*She heaves herself up, the waiter helps her, gives her what she points to.
She writes a few words, begins to laugh.*

ESTER: I feel really fine now, I'll have you know. (*Laughs*)

*She switches on the radio, which at once lets out a searing trumpet-like
sound.*

ESTER: Very pretty. Who'd have thought you have that sort of
music in this nasty little country. D'you know what they
call my condition, old boy? Euphoria. Puts in an appearance
just before the death-throes. It was the same with Father.
He laughed and told funny stories. Then he looked at me:
"Now it's eternity, Ester", he said. He was so kind, though
terribly big and heavy, weighed nearly 400 pounds. I'd like

140

to have seen the faces of the fellows who had to carry the coffin! I'm so tired.

She yawns convulsively, gasps for breath, her eyes become round with terror and a scream rises up from her throat, she lashes about with her arms, trying to get air, leans forward, throws herself back, heaves herself up.

After a few moments the cramps go over.

ESTER (*whispers*):   No, no, no! I don't want to die like that, no, no! I don't want to stifle. Oh, it was horrible! I'm frightened now. It frightened me that time. It mustn't come back. No, no! After all I can't . . .

But the cramps convulse her body. She gapes wide-eyed, her eyes become bloodshot, her complexion darkens.

She sits up straight in bed, her hands over her bosom, her hair all knotted and sweaty, her nose sharp, as if squeezed. Again and again brief attacks of trembling pass through her.

ESTER: Why doesn't the doctor come? (*Pause*) Am I to lie here and die all alone?

The tears well up in her eyes and run down over her cheeks. Like an abandoned child, she weeps helplessly.

The old waiter, utterly at a loss, is standing in the middle of the room, watching her cry. He shakes his head, says something. Then hurries out of the room.

Ester becomes swiftly weaker, her consciousness dims. She calls out, gasping.

ESTER: Mother! I'm ill. Mother, come and help me! I'm so frightened. I'm so frightened. I'm so frightened. I don't want to die.

She stops calling. Listens quietly, stops crying and moaning, pushes away the pillows, lays herself down full-length in the bed.

Pulls the sheet over her face.

Johan, astonished and rather scared, is standing on the threshold. He comes nearer, goes over to the head of the bed.

He hears a watch ticking, fast and hard; turns round. Behind him the old waiter has come in.

Johan lifts the sheet from Ester's face. At once she opens her eyes. Gazes at him a long while.

ESTER (*whispers*):   Don't be scared. I'm not going to die.

JOHAN (*nods silently*).

ESTER: I'm calmer now.

JOHAN: I see.

141

ESTER: I've written you a letter, as I promised. It's lying on the floor, if you can find it. (*Pause*) Johan! It's *important*, d'you understand! You must read it carefully. (*Pause*) It's all . . . It's all I . . . You'll understand.

Her voice is scarcely audible.

Johan begins searching about on the floor, finds the paper with the capital letters and their superscription: TO JOHAN.

Anna goes hastily through the next room. She stops in the doorway.

ANNA: We must hurry. Our train leaves in an hour.

Johan stands by Ester's bed, gazing at her steadily, she gazes at him.

ESTER: Don't be frightened. You must be brave. (*Pause*) You must be brave.

Anna comes in. Her big sweaty body fills the room.

Impatiently she calls her son. But before she can grab him he has dived down to the floor, creeps under the bed.

The old waiter mutters angrily. In a flash he is round at the other side, grabs the boy's arm and draws him out.

Johan stands there, dusty and ruffled. Anna goes up to the bed, but Ester has closed her eyes. A few moments she stands and waits, looks at her sister, bends down over her. Her face close to hers.

ESTER (*weakly*): It's a good thing you're going.

ANNA: No one's asked for your advice.

Anna stands up.

Goes.

Once again Ester and the old man are alone in the stuffy room.

Suddenly a siren begins letting out short dull howls.

The old man closes the window, the agonizing scream dwindles. He glances at the sick woman.

Her face is grey, sunken. Her breath comes in short gasps.

Soundlessly, on tiptoe, he leaves her.

XVI

Darkness is falling over the town.

A poisonous blue-black mass of cloud covers the sky and as the express, shortly after two o'clock, pulls out of the railway yards, the first heavy rain begins to fall.

Anna and Johan are alone in a compartment. Each has a corner seat; neither speaks to the other. She has a book on her knee, but is not reading it. He has taken out Ester's letter and is studying it.

ANNA: What's that?

JOHAN: Ester wrote me a letter.

ANNA (*suspicious*):   A letter. Let's see.

Reluctantly, Johan gives her the crinkled paper with the incomprehensible foreign words.

Anna shrugs, hands it back to her son. He takes it from her and reads it, whispering.

It gets darker and darker, the rain squirts down over the windowpanes. Anna opens the window and lets the water splash over her hands and face. Johan's face is pale with the effort of trying to understand the strange language. This secret message.

Selected List of Grove Press
Drama and Theater Paperbacks

E471   BECKETT, SAMUEL / Cascando and Other Short Dramatic
       Pieces (Words and Music, Film, Play, Come and Go, Eh Joe,
       Endgame) / $1.95
E96   BECKETT, SAMUEL / Endgame / $1.95
E318   BECKETT, SAMUEL / Happy Days / $2.45
E226   BECKETT, SAMUEL / Krapp's Last Tape, plus All That Fall,
       Embers, Act Without Words I and II / $2.45
E33   BECKETT, SAMUEL / Waiting For Godot / $1.95 [See also
       Seven Plays of the Modern Theater, Harold Clurman, ed.
       GT422 / $4.95]
B117   BRECHT, BERTOLT / The Good Woman of Setzuan / $1.95
B108   BRECHT, BERTOLT / Mother Courage and Her
       Children / $1.50
B333   BRECHT, BERTOLT / The Threepenny Opera / $1.45
E130   GENET, JEAN / The Balcony / $2.95 [See also Seven Plays
       of the Modern Theater, Harold Clurman, ed. GT422 / $4.95]
E208   GENET, JEAN / The Blacks: A Clown Show / $2.95
E577   GENET, JEAN / The Maids and Deathwatch:
       Two Plays / $2.95
E374   GENET, JEAN / The Screens / $1.95
E101   IONESCO, EUGENE / Four Plays (The Bald Soprano, The
       Lesson, The Chairs,* Jack, or The Submission) / $1.95
       *[See also Eleven Short Plays of the Modern Theater,
       Samuel Moon, ed. B107 / $2.45]
E259   IONESCO, EUGENE / Rhinoceros* and Other Plays (The
       Leader, The Future is in Eggs, or It Takes All Sorts to Make
       a World) / $1.95 *[See also Seven Plays of the Modern
       Theater, Harold Clurman, ed. GT422 / $4.95]
E119   IONESCO, EUGENE / Three Plays (Amédée, The New
       Tenant, Victims of Duty) / $2.95
B354   PINTER, HAROLD / Old Times / $1.95
E299   PINTER, HAROLD / The Caretaker* and The Dumb Waiter:
       Two Plays / $1.95 *[See also Modern British Drama,
       Henry Popkin, ed. GT422 / $5.95]
E411   PINTER, HAROLD / The Homecoming / $1.95
E626   STOPPARD, TOM / Jumpers / $1.95
B319   STOPPARD, TOM / Rosencrantz and Guilderstern Are
       Dead / $1.95

Grove Press, Inc., 196 West Houston Street, New York, N.Y. 10014